WHILE I REMEMBER

The Life Story of

Ivy Northage

Books by Ivy Northage:

Mediumship Made Simple
Spiritual Realisation
Journey Beyond

WHILE I REMEMBER

The Life Story of

Ivy Northage

Edited by
Brenda Marshall

LIGHT PUBLISHING
At The College of Psychic Studies
LONDON

First published in 1999 by
LIGHT PUBLISHING
At the College of Psychic Studies
16 Queensberry Place
London SW7 2EB

© 1998 The College of Psychic Studies

All rights reserved. No part of this publication may be reproduced, stored in a retrieval system, transmitted in any form or by any means electronic, mechanical, recording or photocopying, or otherwise, without prior permission from the publishers, except for brief quotations embodied in library articles or reviews.

British Library Cataloguing in Publication Data.
A catalogue record for this book is available from the British Library.
ISBN 0 903336 32 4

The aim of LIGHT PUBLISHING at the College of Psychic Studies is to explore all aspects of spiritual and psychic knowledge.

The views expressed in all publications by LIGHT PUBLISHING at the College of Psychic Studies are those of the author and do not necessarily reflect the views of The College of Psychic Studies.

Typeset, printed and bound
in Great Britain by Whitstable
Litho, Whitstable, Kent

Cover design by Pavlou

To The Divine Light of which we are all a part and which both Ivy and Janet served with total dedication

TABLE OF CONTENTS

Page

Introduction

PART I Childhood and Formative Years

1	*A very precocious child. Early disaster. Infancy at the crèche. Childish escapades.*	1
2	*A streetwise childhood. Early psychic intimations. Schooldays.*	15
3	*Theatrical blood in the family. Her mother's childhood and early widowhood. Some psychic experiences.*	27

PART II Marriage and Mediumship

4	*First employment. Marriage and motherhood. First experiments with table-tilting. Launched by 'chance' into psychic work. Her husband's enthusiasm. First visits to Spiritualist meetings.*	35
5	*Reluctantly sitting in the dark. Chan enters their lives. Stanley embarks on a protracted experiment to prove survival. Near-fatal illness of their elder son. They adopt a baby girl.*	49
6	*A demonstration by Estelle Roberts changes Ivy's indifference into genuine dedication. Her training intensified. First appearance on a platform. Is Chan real, she wonders?*	63
7	*Transfiguration. From trance to clairvoyance. A painful lesson from Chan.*	77

8	*Wartime brings a wider field of work and significant new contacts. First experiences of physical demonstrations. A brush with the Salvation Army. In Devon where her sons had been evacuated to a farm. More materialisation seances*	91
9	*Recollections of Helen Duncan. Other remarkable physical mediumship.*	105
10	*Ivy's father and some striking evidence. Materialisations and apports. An embarrassing prank.*	121
11	*Hardships and hazards of travelling in wartime. A near-fatal illness.*	129
12	*Some wartime experiences on tour in Wales. A materialisation seance with Alec Harris.*	141
13	*Some other remarkable mediums; Helen Hughes and Hannah Swaffer. Ivy's mother dies. Her husband is invalided out of the army. Ivy's mediumship begins to gain recognition and she is invited to work at The Spiritualist Association of Great Britain. Janet comes into her life.*	155

PART III Later Years: The Harvest

14	*Ivy declared Medium of the Year at Psychic News annual dinner.*	169
15	*First publication of Chan's trance talks. Some memories of Ivy at The College of Psychic Studies. Reflections on Chan's influence and its effects.*	183
16	*CHAN. Looking back.*	193

INTRODUCTION

When I told Kathleen Raine, the poet, about this book, she wrote: 'I'm so glad to hear that you are working on the memoirs of Ivy Northage, that wonderful woman who has done so much for so many through her God-given gift.'

Ivy Northage was not only one of the most remarkable mediums of her time but the glimpses of her life's experiences which she let fall in private conversation, and sometimes from the platform, left no doubt in those who heard her that her life was of two-fold interest, illustrating the development, hard and sometimes painful, of a most exceptional medium while giving a picture of social conditions long vanished. As she grew older, her many admirers urged her to write down her memoirs so that they would not be lost. This she never did but, fortunately for us, when well into her eighties she started to record her memories on tape. By the time she stopped working, in her eighty-eighth year when illness overtook her, there were fifteen of these tapes and these form the material for this book.

An exceptional degree of independence, courage and generosity of character emerges from her actions, as in the episode of Dolly and her illegitimate babies. These qualities alone would make her a very remarkable human being, apart from her mediumship. But "apart" is a word which cannot properly be used because Ivy lived her beliefs, and although her qualities of character were already clear while she was still a very small child, it was through her mediumship, her work with Chan, his tuition and her lifelong dedication to service under his direction, that her beliefs became the conscious guiding force in her life. Inevitably, with her dominant and uncompromising character, there were times when some people may have found her difficult, but she never, ever, betrayed her own beliefs or went against her own conscience. On her eighty-eighth birthday the floral tributes from friends and admirers transformed her flat into a flower shop and the hundreds of birthday cards stretched in rows across her large sitting room.

What the reader may have the greatest difficulty in believing are the accounts of materialisation phenomena. Indeed Ivy herself said that if she had not seen with her own eyes she could not have believed that these things took place. Discussing with Paul Beard, a notable former President of the College of Psychic Studies, the difficulty of believing what one has not seen - which has always dogged psychical research - he told me that his father attended a seance on a hot day in mid-summer at which a fir tree materialised with snow on its branches. Ivy was privileged to witness an extraordinary range of physical phenomena.

The earlier part of her working life, during and after the second World War, was an era of astonishing physical mediumship, as the latter part of the previous century had been, and the time of the first World War. Many who have made a study of spiritualism in its broadest sense believe this was because, in an age of scientific materialism, feats which seemed to defy the laws of natural science were most likely to challenge disbelief, while the mass bereavement resulting from two world wars gave rise to an urgent need to bring comfort to those left behind by opening their minds to the truth of survival.

At a time when the spirit world was manifesting so dramatically through physical phenomena it seems that earthy, non-mental types of people were the best mediums. It is often asked why we do not see this extraordinary kind of physical mediumship today. Spiritual guides cite the development of society's needs, saying that the tremendous expenditure of power needed to produce such materialisations is not now appropriate, it is better used to promoting spiritual philosophy through mental mediumship. There has, however, been a revival with the founding of the Noah's Ark Society by Robin Foy, a notable physical medium. His recent book on the subject, *In Pursuit of Physical Mediumship*[1], is one of the many titles in the very extensive literature on the subject, notably the classic, *History of Spiritualism*[2] by Sir Arthur Conan Doyle and the *Proceedings* of the Society of Psychical Research. The body of evidence these present makes it hard to avoid conviction.

The strain on the bodies of outstanding physical mediums was intense and often shortened their life. Helen Duncan was a case in point. The controversy surrounding her work has recently been revived in a determination to put the record straight and clear her name. Ivy, while thinking her a rather silly woman in her personal life, had no doubt about the genuineness of her physical mediumship, explaining that what was taken as fraud, because Helen Duncan was seen walking about outside the cabinet, was in fact a lesser degree of physical manifestation because of the medium's depleted vitality. Helen Duncan consistently overworked and was in a state of physical exhaustion.

Alec Harris, whose materialisation phenomena were the most remarkable of all that Ivy witnessed, as they were of many others, had the highest reputation which was never sullied, and he lived to enjoy a normal retirement.

It was usual for physical mediums to work in a cabinet. There was one in the College of Psychic Studies until the refurbishment of the building in 1987 and 1988 when exigencies of space necessitated its removal. Although Ivy had long ceased to demonstrate transfiguration, it was in this room that she worked for so many years.

Her memories were not all in chronological order, nor was her memory for dates and subsidiary details as sharp as it had been, but during the months when I was writing her story, as well as through the whole of these last years, I regularly spent hours with her, talking over these and other matters. Though she was then in constant pain, her mind was clear and focused and in these talks she expanded and elaborated on what she had dictated, so that this is indeed her own story.

Brenda Marshall
May 1998

[1] *London, Janus Publishing 1996. ISBN 1 85756 248 8*
[2] *Reprinted 1997, Psychic Press, London.*

CHAPTER 1

A very precocious child. Early disaster. Infancy at the crèche. Childish escapades.

You had to be seven to join the children's library but this little girl could not wait two years. Tottering up the steps on tiny legs and mustering all her resolution, in she went and across to a desk where she saw three grown-ups in attendance. Some instinct prompted her to stand in front of the man with a beard. He leant over and looked down at her. The top of her head barely came up to the level of the desk.

'Well?'

'I've come to join the library.'

'How old are you?'

'Seven,' she said.

The man took a long, hard look at her. Then he picked up a book and opened it in front of her.

'Read that.'

Her precocious love of reading was why she needed to join the library. With no difficulty at all she read the page through. When she had finished,

'You're seven,' he said.

Not only did this understanding and kindly man enrol her in the library but from then on he took a special interest in her progress, guiding her reading and stimulating her already very active mind and imagination, helping them to unfold and fostering her considerable natural gifts.

There are many such examples which illustrate how Ivy Northage's childhood, outwardly one of extreme deprivation, in fact provided her with a better education for her life's vocation than she could have come by in any other way. When, at the end of her life, she looked back on her early years she could see how all the factors contributed directly to making her the medium she became. Just how great her mediumship was did not seem to occur to her. She remained extremely modest about her gift, emphasising only that once she had made her commitment, her dedication to the call of spirit had been total, in her middle years sometimes coming before the claims of her marriage.

Ivy Fitzpatrick, – christened Margaret, because the Catholic priest rejected 'Ivy', which her parents had chosen, as not being a proper name – was born on 10th July 1909 in Middlesbrough. On their marriage her parents had gone there from London as her father had a job in the steelworks. Her father was Irish and her mother half Italian. Her brother, born in the first year of their marriage, was two years older. When Ivy was three months old her father was killed in an accident at work. In those days any payment of compensation was nominal. (Ivy's recollection from what her mother told her is £200.) Her mother, virtually destitute, returned to London. There, apart from some early assistance from her own and her husband's relatives, themselves in very straitened circumstances, she was faced with the responsibility of providing for herself and her two year-old son and infant daughter.

Life was extremely hard in 1909. There were no welfare benefits, nothing to support families in poverty except charity. Because her mother was obliged to work for very long hours from Ivy's infancy, she hardly knew her during those early years and what she knows is either from her own direct memories or from talks with her mother many years later. Her mother was a beautiful woman and could well have remarried but, as she told Ivy many years afterwards, she was afraid a stepfather might not care for her children as she was determined to do.

She found herself a job in Crosse and Blackwells factory, which was then where the Astoria is now in Tottenham Court Road. But how to provide for her son, aged two, and Ivy, not yet one, during the very long working hours of those days? The solution was the crèche run by the Methodist Church in Kingsway Hall where mothers could leave their children from 7.30 in the morning until 6.00 in the evening.

One of Ivy's earliest recollections from before she could walk but which remained indelibly clear in her mind, was of herself in a pushchair being handed over a dividing door – the half doors customarily used in stables – and looking into a large lighted room with pink-covered cots around a large space in the centre. This was the babies' room. You stayed there until you were two when you were moved to what was called the day room. This was the kindergarten.

Only when she came to look back on her life did Ivy appreciate the significance of those early years and understand how fortunate she was, for that kindergarten was run on the then very new Montessori methods, something she could never have hoped to benefit from except through the most enlightened charity. This was effectively her home for the first and most formative five years of her life. She still remembers the attractive way in which things were taught, all designed to encourage and stimulate. You learned to lace your shoes on huge frames of brightly coloured leather pierced with holes. There were attractive fabrics with buttons and buttonholes. In what seemed like play with these, you learned to button your clothes. Thinking back to those days, Ivy could see with hindsight how privileged she was, paradoxical as it might seem. All the early teaching she received was designed, in her words, 'to make you aware of your own capacity for independence'.

The extraordinary degree to which independence and self-reliance were Ivy's most notable characteristics from a very early age becomes apparent from her own recollections. These start from her infancy with affectionate memories of the crèche and kindergarten at their Methodist Church headquarters in Kingsway Hall.

Ivy recollects:
It was a large room, as I remember it, with kitchens and other rooms leading off. We were on the top floor. Below was the enormous Kingsway Hall in which the Sunday services and other adult activities were held. Sister Hope looked after us in the crèche, while others had their own tasks and responsibilities. The Sisters were all housed in their own bed-sitting rooms on, I think, the third floor. Below that was yet another floor with lesser halls, one of which was called the Oak Room, in which, as I grew older, we attended Sunday School.

It was a kind of enormous home to me from those early years of awakening ideas and thoughts and so, of course, it was the formation of my character and understanding. I have no knowledge of home as 'home' in those first five years, other than being taken in a pushchair, early each morning, then later being held by the hand for the ten minutes walk from Theobald's Road, where I lived, to Kingsway and the crèche. And then coming home at night.

I remember very vividly an incident in thick snow. We were going through Red Lion Square which was covered in snow, my brother holding on at the side and my mother pushing me in the pushchair, when suddenly the whole thing collapsed. I tipped forward onto the ground, the wheel came off the pushchair, my poor mother went down on her knees and my brother, of course, fell down too. We were all lying in a heap and I can remember this so well because of the coldness of the snow on my face. I presume I was yelling madly but I do remember my mother's distress.

A lady came up and just stood there, making no offer to help. My mother told me years later that she looked down at her slumped in the snow and said,

'Oh, you poor soul. Have you fallen down?'

To which my mother retorted,

'Oh, no, I do this regularly for a living.' (Her mother had been an actress.) My mother's sharp wit was a subsequent joy, though sadly, only in recollection, as I never truly appreciated it while she was still with me.

These first five years were ones of learning a rich variety of things and of being taught how to stand upon my own two feet. We were taught to memorise, to recite and sing, regularly being taken down to the great hall to perform there, often with an audience. (I could still recite the hymns and poems we learned all those years ago.) Every April a sale of work was held to raise funds for the crèche. Stalls were set up in the great hall and we children in our little blue crèche uniforms were sent out into Kingsway holding little bunches of primroses to sell to passers-by. An adult accompanied us to take the money but it was we who sold the primroses.

On another occasion it was instilled into us that a famous and beautiful princess was coming to visit us. I can't remember where she came from but people from various countries used to visit us because of the very modern system by which we were being taught. Interested people from overseas were eager to see the method in practice. To prepare us for this visit we were lined up and shown how to curtsy.

'When the lady comes through the door,' we were told, 'you hold your skirts like this, then you just bend your knees and bow your head. You must do it very nicely.'

As two, three and four year-olds we were very near the ground anyway and we practised in our playroom and became quite proficient. Finally four of us were chosen to greet the princess, presumably the ones who were most confident. Certainly I was chosen and when the great day came, there we were, lined up at the doorway waiting for the princess to arrive. We had been practising in the centre of our playroom and it had not entered my head that when we were lined up at the door we would be directly in front of the five fire buckets that were always kept filled with water, just inside the door.

The lady came in, looking very graciously at these tiny tots waiting to curtsy to her. I obediently did mine, but my bottom got stuck in the fire bucket. I can still remember being most indignant about this and yelling with rage and discomfort. Years later my mother told me there was a picture in that evening's paper of the princess, bending down and laughing uncontrollably while trying to extricate me from the bucket.

While I was still in the nursery crèche, Sister Hope, knowing my mother's circumstances, arranged for me to be sent away for short holidays in the summer. One was to Pevensey Bay of which I remember only the name. But I can still recall the feeling of desolation that overcame me on a train to Brighton, sitting in a railway carriage and seeing those cliffs that come into view just before you arrive. As the train passed along there, within sight of those big cliffs, I began to cry. I did not know why I was crying, but it must have been my first experience of homesickness and it indicates that, grim and sparse as the conditions of my home life were, the security of familiar surroundings and being with my mother, however briefly, mattered to me very much.

We were put to sleep in very large beds – single beds, but they were very big. At home I slept with my mother and I can remember waking up regularly on the floor underneath the bed until they found me a cot. These holidays were for two weeks. At the end of the first week we were taken to meet the oncoming party and to take those now going back home to the station, and I remember wishing that it was my week to go home. I have pondered on this since, because they were quite kind to me there. But there was a longing for things familiar which I have never lost, even now. I like things with which I am familiar. I know that I am not a person for change.

I have few clear recollections of being with my brother in those early days, except that he was supposed to look after me after school. He was two years older, but that was still very young. I remember he would dump me somewhere, telling me to stay there while he went off to play with his friends. Boys and girls were very strictly segregated in those days. I would be on someone's doorstep and usually fell fast asleep. My mother told me later that he did not always remember where he had left me and she, almost distraught, would demand,

'Well, where did you leave her last?'

One memorable scrape we got into together we managed to keep from her completely. She worked hard for very long hours all during the week, and on Sunday afternoons she sent us off to Sunday School in Kingsway Hall. No-one accompanied us on our walk there from Theobald's Road and after Sunday School my brother would take me anywhere that took his fancy. Free of restrictions as our unsupervised life left us, our imagination and our uncurbed personalities found expression in any way they could. I would have been four or five when my brother decided to go down to the river. From Kingsway we went to the Strand and then down through those turnings that led to the river. It was summer and I was in a white dress with white socks and shoes. I don't remember what my brother was wearing but my mother would always send us out looking as nice as she could. The steps down to the edge of the water were rather steep and slippery for me, but I managed, and my brother said,

'Let's have a paddle.'

'We can't,' I protested. 'We can't take our shoes and socks off.'

'Oh, yes, we can,' he said. 'We'll tie them together and hang them round our necks.'

So we took off our socks and shoes. He helped me to tie mine and put them round my neck, and we stepped into the water. But instead of meeting solid ground, our feet sank into soft mud. He, being taller and stronger and no doubt more alert to the danger, just managed to pull back onto the bottom step, safe himself but out of reach of my hand. I, meanwhile, a little ahead of him, was rapidly sinking into the mud. It was already over the hem of my dress and I was screaming my head off because my legs were stuck and I could not move. A man who had seen what was happening came rushing down the steps, held out his arm for my hand and literally dragged me out of the mud, which in those few moments was up to my waist.

By now my dress was covered in slimy grey mud and over my sobs I could hear this man telling my brother off for allowing such a thing to happen. Eventually we all climbed up the steps and came to a ladies' public lavatory. This man had taken charge of us by now and told my brother to go in and ask the attendant if she would help. Very reluctantly he went down the steps to the entrance and called out to the attendant. She came out to see what it was all about, took one look at my sorry state, dripping wet and covered with mud, and came hurrying over to help. She was very stout and certainly most kind. I remember her telling my brother to go and sit on the top step and wait. She took me in her arms and stripped me completely, including all my underwear, which, of course, was stained with mud. She washed all those things and somehow she dried them. She dried my dress and my vest and my knickers and she ironed them, and when they were ready she dressed me again. My socks and shoes had been around my neck so these were not spoiled.

Neither I nor my brother ever told my mother what had happened and she never knew how near we had come to tragedy. Nor, I am sure, did she realise that my brother was quite incorrigible about these escapades.

'We are going on an adventure,' he would say, and I would trot along with him because there was nowhere else for me to go.

Sadly, my brother did get himself into bad company and my mother was extremely worried. She talked about it to Sister Hope who was always a great support. Sister Hope told her about the National Children's Home, a Methodist establishment, and while they did not normally take children with parents, they might make an exception in my brother's case. When he was nine and I was seven he went to live in the Home.

I don't remember learning to read. In my recollection I could always read. At five years old we had to leave the crèche and go to the elementary school. I must have shown a great deal of disdain when I was patiently introduced to the alphabet and this did not make me popular. I was also meeting older children now and some of them talked about books they had borrowed from a public library. This possible access to a wider range of reading had a tremendous appeal for me but when I asked about it the children jeered. (I was not popular at school.)

'You can't join,' they said, 'You have to be seven.'

By now my habit of self-reliance was firmly established and I determined to find the place on my own.

Everything was in the vicinity of Holborn and Kingsway, all my early life centres around that particular square mile. The library was in Holborn, just beside the very famous Holborn restaurant, which, like all the old landmarks I remember, alas, is no longer there. I found my way there and walked into another high-ceilinged building, past walls lined with books, to a long desk behind which sat two or three library staff, and approached the man with a grey beard and very bright blue eyes. With hindsight I cannot help feeling that I was guided to choose this particular one because he was to have a very important and formative guiding role in my development over the next few years.

There were no school dinners in those days and I used to go back to the crèche for mine. Sister Hope had arranged this for my mother, realising that we still needed a great deal of assistance. She did not finish work until the evening, seven-thirty if I remember correctly, and there was nowhere for me to go after school. I could go back to the crèche, they still allowed me that, but I could no longer take part in the crèche activities. I could wander around the building, but there was nothing for me to do. When it was cold I was glad to find a warm spot and sit and read my books but in summer I used to wander around the streets, playing with children from school until their mothers called them in for tea around half past five or six o'clock. The only sense of deprivation I recall from those days was a rather desolate feeling when they had gone and I was left with no-one to call me home. I remember it as a slight pang, a slight ache when I wished that I, too, could have been called home, that there was someone I could go home to. But I don't remember it as a trauma and it sowed the seeds of tremendous self-reliance.

Left alone, I would curl myself up in a corner and read my book. Sadly for me in those days, if you finished a book you could not take it back the same day. As I had two or three hours to fill in each day it did not take me long to read my book and I would dearly have loved to be able to go back and change it. So I was left with quite a bit of time to get through, and my natural curiosity combined with my growing resourcefulness to lead me into all kinds of adventures.

My boundaries at this time were that small area of the West End with the greatest concentration of cinemas, theatres and music halls. I had no money but I was very observant, and in my wanderings I noticed that these places had back entrances which might enable me to bypass the person who always stood there taking money and giving out tickets. In Tottenham Court Road, where I used to go every evening to meet my mother when she came out of Crosse and Blackwells, I passed a cinema, and one afternoon I slipped in through the back door. Inside, I saw a door to the toilets and another one which I squeezed through, and found myself in the cinema. It was quite dark in there and I managed to creep in and find myself a seat where I watched a film which held me enthralled. Full of anticipation, I made my way there the next day, only to find the programme was the same. So I remembered that there was another cinema up the road and I used to do the round of the cinemas, entertaining myself and keeping out of the cold.

Just how these exploits reveal not only Ivy's natural qualities of character but also the way in which the circumstances of her childhood were exactly those best calculated to develop the gifts she brought to her life's work becomes increasingly clear as her story unfolds. Already, before the age of five, she had the confidence and the initiative to pursue her goal, together with a complete absence of shyness or any kind of embarrassment when asked to sing or recite before an audience.

CHAPTER 2

A streetwise childhood. Early psychic intimations. Schooldays.

Most of these experiences occurred accidentally. I was not seeking them, often they just happened, and because they did it made me more alert to other possibilities. The Holborn Empire was situated behind the main road, reached through a little alley backing onto Lincoln's Inn Fields and I found it quite accidentally while wandering around Holborn. It wasn't visible from the main road. People arriving had to alight in Holborn and walk through into the Empire. Happening to be in that particular spot on one occasion, I saw a taxi draw up and a very well-dressed lady get out. The driver opened the door for her and as he closed it behind her and she walked across the little entrance into the alleyway, he called out,

'Tata, Marie, be back for yer in 'alf an hour.'

It was the famous Marie Lloyd and, as I learned later, artistes used to go from one music hall to another, appearing in three or even four in one evening. There were two houses a night. The artistes arranged for their taxis to pick them up and they would change in the taxi, adjusting their make-up to fit the next turn.

I had heard of Marie Lloyd, who was extremely famous in

her day, so I followed, and saw her ignore the main entrance of the Empire and enter by a small side door. By now I was very interested in side doors and I followed her through into a small corridor-like space with two outlets. One went up a flight of stairs which Marie took, presumably to her dressing room, but the other let me into the theatre auditorium, parallel with the orchestra. In those days the orchestra was in a pit, below the level of the stage, and curtained off. This screening was slightly above my height and I found that if I hid myself behind the curtain I could be quite invisible to anyone in the auditorium and still have an excellent view of the stage. The performance was well under way; Marie, being the star, did not have to arrive at the beginning. To watch a live performance was yet another new and rich experience for me.

When I have talked to other mediums, most have said they had psychic experiences in their early, formative years. I did not, certainly not in any dramatic or obvious way and only long afterwards did I recognise anything psychic in some of my memories. The Holborn Empire, as I have explained, was not visible from the main road so there was an advertising board in Holborn. Walking past with my mother on one occasion I saw Marie Lloyd's name there. For no reason I was aware of, I turned to my mother and said,

'She's going to die.'

'Of course,' said my mother, ' We're all going to die eventually.'

'Oh no,' I replied, 'She is going to die soon.'

My mother looked at me a little strangely and let the subject drop. The next week, from Holborn, Marie went to Wood Green Empire, where she collapsed and died.

Another flash I recall I see clearly now was of a psychic nature. A school teacher whom I remember with great kindness, announced one morning that she was going to take us that afternoon to Epping Forest. I went home, knowing my mother would be there. This was unheard of, and whether she had time off or there was short time at the factory I have no idea, but there she was. Somehow she had come by a piece of material and had been making me a dress which she finished just as I arrived. I knew she was going to be there, though I certainly did not anticipate the dress. I was able to wear it for the outing in the afternoon and the joy of that occasion stays with me as a real highlight.

Not all my recollections are of happy times. I remember watching my mother writhing with agony with neuritis in her leg and wondering what on earth to do. She was crying out, the pain was so bad, and she was unable to get from her chair to the bed. I was seven at the time and had never felt so utterly helpless. I remember the neighbour upstairs coming down and insisting on sending for a doctor. And then being sent off to school next day and coming home – I can see it now – to an empty bed, the bedclothes all turned back. They told me she had been taken to hospital and she was there for about a month. I got myself to school each day and I got myself home. This is my most enduring recollection of having to stand alone on my own two feet.

I had my own experience of being in hospital when I was nine. Vividly, I remember being knocked down by a donkey cart, the wheels running over my ankles, myself lying helpless in the road, and the two large men in charge of the cart running away. A policeman took me to the casualty ward of the old Charing Cross Hospital, then in Charing Cross. My ankles were not broken but so badly sprained that I could not walk. They bandaged me up but you had to pay for hospitals in those days so they discharged me, offering no help in how I was to get home. They must have sent for my mother. I remember it took four hours for me to limp there, after which the pain and the injuries to my ankles were so bad I could not move. My mother could not look after me as she was working all day so I was sent to the free hospital in Highbury. I think I was there for a fortnight and as I was quite well apart from the fact that I could not walk I remember it very clearly.

It was a huge ward with smaller side wards and an area with tables for those who could move around. I was terrified of mice because we were overrun with them at home, but lying there in bed with the sun pouring in at sunset – the evenings were very long – I could see the mice running about under the tables and I amused myself by watching them at play.

Opposite was a very old lady with a loud voice and the nurses used to joke with her. They washed her with no screens at all and somehow I realised that this was an afront to natural dignity. I never, ever saw my mother undressed, even though our arrangements at home were so primitive, and in some obscure way this mattered.

There is another vivid cameo from when I began to be able to walk. On my way to the bathroom I looked in at a side ward and saw a woman lying, like a wax effigy, absolutely flat on her bed. I had never seen a dead person but somehow I knew that she was very near death. Our eyes met and something passed between us. That registered in a way I did not understand but I can see it now. I think I was then brought face to face with the finality of life. Back in bed, perhaps half an hour later, I saw them wheeling out her tiny form covered with a sheet.

Why these pictures remain in my mind so vividly is that they reflect stages in my awakening as an individual. I can see now that everything I did was precocious, sometimes with a sense of mischief, but underneath, gradually unfolding, was the assertion of myself as a person. My totally unrestricted life, the complete absence of forms of discipline or restraint, released in me the uninhibited development of my own thoughts. There was no-one to guide me, no-one with whom I could share my thoughts. I used to ponder a great many things but all my questions were addressed to myself. I was very firm in my own beliefs and nothing incensed me more than injustice. I did not throw tempers when things upset me but withdrew into myself. I would run away into a corner, find privacy within myself, and if I did not want to talk about something nobody could make me. On one such occasion our class had been told to write about Ireland in the context of the troubles at the time which must often have featured in the newspapers. I knew absolutely nothing about the subject except that my father had been Irish and in some obscure way I could not accept the prevailing hostility to the Irish cause. It seemed to me wrong that girls who knew nothing about it should be asked to express an opinion and I flatly refused to do it. This caused quite a scene in the classroom but I stood my ground and eventually was sent to the Headmistress to be disciplined. She, however, listened carefully when I explained why I could not write about Ireland. Recognising my sincerity, she set me a different subject. I was often called defiant or disobedient, but for me it was an intense need to maintain my own integrity.

I was very fortunate to be living in Bloomsbury and to be going to school there, because that area of London was the heart of a great deal of the culture of the time; theatres, music halls, concerts, cinemas, all were concentrated in that square mile. Life at school became more interesting with a Headmistress who was a Shakespearean scholar and a music teacher devoted to Gilbert and Sullivan. From our school in Kingsway it was a short walk over Waterloo Bridge to The Old Vic where we were taken regularly to see the most wonderful performances of Shakespeare's plays. Although not competent to appreciate them fully in those schooldays, I must have seen all the classic productions with the major performers of the day, a standard of excellence which undoubtedly influenced me profoundly and had its effect in later years when I came to appear on the platform as a medium.

The very first play I saw was " As You Like It". I remember this because the opening scene so frightened me. I had only just moved up from the Infants School so I would not have been more than seven or eight and while I was quite familiar with music hall and pantomime I had never seen straight theatre. This wrestling scene, with one actor fighting so realistically against another, then lifting him up and throwing him over his shoulder when he lay prone on the floor, shocked and terrified me.

The gallery at The Old Vic where we would sit was just wooden benches with no backs and wooden boards underfoot. I believe the price was 3d, three old pennies. It was extremely well supported by the public. One of my still vivid recollections is the solo monologues of Bransbury Williams, the most famous of which is The Bells, but I particularly loved those devoted to Charles Dickens. He would devote a whole afternoon's performance, two and a half or three hours, to characters and scenes from Dickens. Even his face seemed to take on the contours of the part he was playing. There he was on stage in front of you. He would turn around and put on this hat, or that wig, turn again, and he was a different person; he seemed to make his face fatter or thinner according to the character.

Our very enlightened Headmistress and the enthusiasm of our music teacher stimulated and awakened me to new sides of myself. I had a good natural singing voice. Training, to my regret, was out of the question through lack of money, but had I been trained, I know that I might have accomplished something as a singer. I sang in Sunday School and took on solo roles in the Gilbert and Sullivan performances organised by the school. Side by side with this new creative outlet I was introduced in the best possible way to the magic of Shakespeare, something which has never left me. The Headmistress would appear with a volume of the plays and, after announcing which one we were going to perform, would tell us that anyone who memorised a part could play it.

This for me opened up vistas of showing off, a wonderful outlet for all that was inside me seething for expression. The beauty of the language, the music of the words, made an indelible impression long before I understood their meaning. All this time my friend at the library was nourishing my imagination and my literary taste by suggesting different authors for me to read during these formative years. The only one I recall specifically now is Dickens. For me, he painted pictures and with my highly imaginative tendency I identified with his characters as I read about them. My mother, too, loved to read when she could find a spare moment, but she, always overworked and always worried about money, sought escape in light fiction; Ethel M. Dell, I remember, a popular romantic novelist of the time, and Rider Haggard. I did not much care for these but nevertheless I devoured her books as well. All this was being laid down in my subconscious mind which provided a foundation of words and images on which I could draw many years later in my work as a medium, when Chan explained to me that he depended for the expression of his thoughts on the words already in my vocabulary; he used these like the keys of a typewriter.

My mother and I used to go to the Royal parks to watch official processions. In the summer of 1919 we went to join in the elaborate Peace Celebrations staged that year with a most spectacular display of fireworks. There was no control of the huge crowds surging in both directions afterwards and my mother and I, trying to get out, were nearly trampled underfoot. We were saved by a man who pulled me in between himself and my mother, put his arms around her waist and the other under my armpits and managed to hold us up, piloting us along until eventually we got out. Later we learned from the publicity that twelve people were crushed to death in the crowd.

I would have been about twelve or thirteen when the new County Hall was completed and I remember being taken from school to the official opening by Princess Mary, then heavily pregnant with Viscount Lascelles. My mother had taken me to watch her wedding procession but this time what struck me was that she looked so unhappy. My brother was now living in the children's home at Bramholt, very close to the Lascelles estate and there were rumours about the marriage. Young as I was, this was yet another facet of life which I took in.

Sister Hope had been a true friend to us all since my days in the crèche. When she inherited from her brother a large house in Barnet, which was still quite in the country then, she decided to turn it into a holiday home for children from the crèche. She had kept in touch all the time I was at school and thought of me now. Saying that I had grown up to be quite useful and responsible, she asked if I would help with the work of getting the house ready. With hindsight, I think this was further kindness on her part. At any rate, I was sent along with the senior nurse from the crèche who went to prepare the house. She was the most charming woman who had been widowed in the First World War and she made it a home for me while I was there. I helped her as much as I possibly could and for the first time in my life I enjoyed an ordered existence with regular meals and realised what it would be like to have a proper home. Until then I had been aware of this lack more vaguely as something missing in the background of my life. This new experience showed me a positive aspect and sowed seeds of domesticity which later mattered to me so much and which, I think now, were responsible for my marrying so young.

There was only one teacher at school who was understanding or sympathetic to me. In the main I was ostracised by those in authority, I suppose because I was so precocious and because of what, in their eyes, was my bad behaviour, though it was really because I did not know any better. I well remember my first contact with this teacher, I was not in her class then. We would assemble in the playground before going in after play and I used to get the most violent headaches; they were in fact migraines, though I did not know that until later. Different teachers took playground duty, and this one stopped by me and asked if I was feeling all right. When I told her I had a very bad headache she said I should go home.

'I can't,' I said. 'My mother is at work and there is no-one at home.'

'What do you do all day?' she asked.

'I go back to the crèche for my dinner and come back to school.'

'I'll give you a note,' she said. 'Take it back to your crèche and ask them to take care of you until your mother comes home.'

That was the first act of kindness at school I had ever known. I never forgot it. On another occasion we were taken to sing carols and this same teacher asked for volunteers to sing the page in Good King Wenceslas. I put my hand up and sang it.

'What a pretty voice,' she said, with the same kindness. 'Couldn't you have lessons?' When I said no, it was not possible, my mother had no money, 'Never mind', she said. 'You will give a lot of pleasure singing as you do.'

That teacher never had any trouble with me. I would have done anything for her. I was thirteen when she left to get married. She married an architect and lived quite close because we had left Bloomsbury by then and moved to Highbury. I was devastated when she left but when I discovered she was living in Highbury I wrote to her. How did I find out her address? By intrepidly following her home on one occasion.

She kept in touch and invited me to her home to tea when her first child was born. She had two little girls, then a boy, rather quickly, only about eighteen months or two years between them.

On the last occasion, when I wrote to say I was getting married, she had just come back from having her third and last child, which had given her a very bad time. She was not young to marry and have children and the assistance in those days was not so good. But in her kindness she invited me to tea and I remember she looked awfully ill. Hers was the first real kindness and friendship I had known in a personal way. I always remember when her last boy was born because it was two weeks before I myself was married.

It was through my love of singing that I came to know my husband. His father owned a butcher's shop in Red Lion passage off Red Lion Square and my mother used to buy meat there. The family lived over the shop. I must have seen Stanley playing in the street as a child because it was like a village around there. The Northage family were musical. In those days there were a great many working men's clubs and they held regular concerts. Stanley would be engaged to sing at these and his brother Arthur, a brilliant pianist, would be invited to accompany the artistes.

One day when I went into the shop, Mrs Northage, who of course knew me quite well by sight, asked if I was interested in music and told me her sons were taking part in a fundraising Gilbert and Sullivan concert at the Conservative Club. I enjoyed this concert immensely and enquired from Mrs Northage when the next one would be held, whereupon she invited me to join the family at the private musical evenings they held each Wednesday. The opportunity these evenings afforded me to sing was a great joy. I also sang quite often at the Kingsway Hall.

CHAPTER 3

Theatrical blood in the family. Her mother's childhood and early widowhood. Some psychic experiences.

I had some theatrical blood in my veins; my grandmother was on the stage as a girl. By the time I knew her she was a rather strange character. When I was a child we lived in the same house, she in the back room and we in the front one. I never did know why she and my mother could not get on, but quite definitely they did not. My grandmother never helped domestically in any way with myself or my brother but she did take us to the cinema from time to time. What I really remember is the enthralling way she would tell me stories about her own youth. This, indeed, had been romantic. She never mentioned her own parents, from whom she had been estranged. She had a brother living in Newcastle who owned a dairy but he never visited us when he came to London. Anything I knew about him I learned through my mother.

But it was my grandmother's life which captured my imagination. As a child she lived with her grandmother who owned a fishing fleet in Newcastle and was quite wealthy. My grandmother trained for the stage at a very early age and at sixteen was playing in the theatre in Newcastle, in repertory, and at Christmas she appeared in pantomime as Prince

Charming. She had lost her looks by the time I knew her but she had been very beautiful as I saw from a portrait she treasured, painted when she was young. It showed her in a splendid evening dress of blue silk with sleeves which, in the style of the time, fell away over her soft, young arms like draperies. But it was her hair which was so striking; thick and golden and gleaming, piled up luxuriantly on the top of her head and circled by a tiara.

It was when she was appearing in the theatre in Newcastle that she met the man she was eventually to marry. It was love at first sight with him. He came round to the stage door after the performance to wait for her and his courtship started then. He was one of a well-to-do Italian family of bankers and hotel owners. They had just successfully launched a big hotel in Naples and wanting to expand into England, had sent him to learn the English side of the business. He declared his intention at once, explaining at the same time that he could not introduce her to his family as his chosen bride until she had received an education which would fit her for Italian society. She must have fallen very much in love with him because she agreed to his sending her away for three years to a finishing school in Italy, where she learned not only Italian but French, along with the arts of deportment and social graces. He then married her and took her to be presented to his family in Rome.

All this enthralled me as a child but the sequel was not so rosy. He had four or five brothers who later disowned him because, as my grandmother learned to her cost, he was the black sheep of the family, a drunkard and something of a reprobate, never faithful to his wife. He later developed tuberculosis and my grandmother took him to Brighton in the hope of restoring his health but the climate did not suit him. He should have gone back to Italy but by now he had lost all their money and he was reduced, at first, to being a head waiter in one hotel or another, and then to any hotel job he could get. In London in those days waiters looking for work would stand about outside the hotels and the managers would come out and choose as many as were required for the evening. Before he was reduced to this indignity he had been for a time Head Waiter at the Café Royal, then in its heyday, and had known Oscar Wilde and the Marquess of Queensberry and other notables of the time.

I never knew my grandfather. He was much older than my grandmother and died when he was only fifty-two, so I would hardly have been born.

My grandmother had thirteen children, only two of whom survived. There seems little doubt that my grandfather had contracted venereal disease. My mother was one of triplets and for the first three months of her precarious life she had to be carried around on a cushion. In these earlier days of their marriage my grandparents were constantly travelling on business connected with the hotels in Venice and elsewhere in Italy and my mother was deemed too delicate to be taken with them. She was sent to live with my grandmother's sister, the wife of a wealthy man with a large house in Finsbury Park. This couple had no children of their own and the husband, particularly, adored my mother and gave her a loving home. He would play with her and in the evening would bring her home some kind of present. To everyone's shock and dismay, when she was about five, my mother became blind. The loss of her sight persisted for about two years until one day she told her nanny, 'I can see my fingers, but they are all black.' At first she could only see shadows but gradually her sight came back, although she always had a certain amount of trouble with her eyes.

Just as she was rejoicing at the return of her sight, another blow befell my mother. The man who had been a father to her died. This left her desolate but worse was to come. The widow remarried and her new husband did not want this child, who was sent back to live with her parents. Meanwhile my grandmother had borne the other of her two children who survived, another daughter, four years younger than my mother, whom they doted on. One can imagine the jealousy between the sisters and the unhappy time my mother experienced. Altogether, I think she had a pretty raw deal.

Although my mother would never have thought of herself as psychic, she did have some experiences of psychic intervention. During her pregnancy with me, although quite unaware of it at the time, she was witness to the precognition of the tragedy that changed her life.

After their marriage, she and my father were living in Middlesbrough in rented rooms above their landlady, a practising clairvoyant with people constantly calling to consult her. My mother, a staunch Catholic, would have nothing to do with this; in fact she was rather uneasy about it and just before I was due to be born she told my father she wanted to leave.

In those days you could just go out and find somewhere. My mother found a little house, very small and humble, but one she decided she would like. The front door opened directly into the living room, there was a scullery at the back and the bedroom above. When she came back after agreeing with the landlord that she would take it, she was met by her landlady who greeted her with,

'Have you found somewhere to live?'

My mother was a bit embarrassed because she had not yet mentioned her intention of moving.

'Well, yes, I have found two rooms with a bit more space than we have here,' she said. 'A little house.'

She was on fairly friendly terms with the landlady who expressed a wish to see the place, so one day, during the preparations for the move, my mother took her there.

The slate and brick floor had been covered with linoleum, which often leaves a musty, rather unpleasant smell when it is removed. When this clairvoyant walked over the front step of the room, she took one look and fainted. My mother was terribly upset. She thought it must have been the rather musty smell because the place had been empty for some time. That was a month before I was born, and they duly moved in.

When I was three months old my father was killed in an accident at work. Coming round to express her sympathy, the former landlady said,

'Do you remember the first time you showed me the house?'

'Of course I do,' replied my mother.

'You know why I fainted?'

'I thought it was the smell of the room.'

'No', replied the lady. 'As I stepped over the threshold the window at the back of the house was opposite the front door, and in that window I saw your husband's coffin.'

Now that was extraordinary in itself because a coffin would almost invariably be placed in the centre of the room so that people coming to pay their respects could walk round it, and my father's body had not yet been brought home. The coffin was due the following day and my mother's next door neighbour, wishing to spare her extra distress, suggested she should wait in her house until it was settled in place. My mother took advantage of this kindly offer and did not return until the undertaker had left. And there was the coffin, placed, against all normal custom, in the window.

This same medium was at the centre of another significant episode. After my father's death my mother returned to London but a few years later she made a trip to Middlesbrough to see her old friends, taking my brother and me by coastal steamer because it was the cheapest way to travel. My mother felt she could not look up her friends without calling on her former landlady. This lady expressed no surprise at seeing her, but said at once,
'I'm so glad you have come. Harry' (my father) 'has been here all week. I am to tell you that the little girl is fine but the little boy is very ill and you must get medical attention.'
Now my brother at that time was running around like the four-year-old he was and my mother was not at all pleased. Her visit was very short because she could not afford to be away from work for long. At sea, on the way home, somewhere along Teesside, my brother became ill. He was taken off the ship as an emergency and rushed to the nearest hospital where measles with complications was the diagnosis, and my mother and I had to stay with him until he was fit to

travel. If she had not been alerted to the seriousness of his illness she would almost certainly not have agreed for us all to be taken off the ship.

I have few psychic recollections of my own childhood. Possibly these did not register at the time, or they have been overlaid by my later experience, but one still vivid in my mind is of a psychic contact with my father whom I had never met. I was seven when, after a routine school inspection, it was seen that I needed dental work and an appointment for this was arranged with a dentist. There was no-one to go with me, my mother, as always being at the factory, so I had to go alone. The work entailed being given gas (dental anaesthetics were more primitive then) and what I remember so clearly, while still under the effects of the gas, is of not wanting to come back; and then being aware of my father and hearing his gentle voice, kindly but firm, telling me I must go back.

How did I know it was my father? I can only say I *knew*, and his communications with me in later life confirmed that I was right.

CHAPTER 4

First employment. Marriage and motherhood. First experiments with table-tilting. Launched by 'chance' into psychic work. Her husband's enthusiasm. First visits to Spiritualist meetings.

After leaving school I went to work in Novello's, the music publishers in Bond Street. This was where my mother had worked before her marriage when she had to leave, because married women were not employed. Such a rule was not observed quite so rigidly after the First World War (although throughout the 1930s and until the outbreak of the Second World War banks, for instance, did not employ married women) and my mother had gone back to her old employment which was a good deal easier and more pleasant than the factory. It was through her that I was taken on and apprenticed to learn bookbinding.

During these years Stanley and I had been brought together by our love of music and of singing and when I was eighteen I agreed to marry him. We were married in the small chapel at the Methodist Headquarters at Kingsway Hall which had been home for me for so much of my early life. I had expected a very quiet occasion but to my amazement the large hall was filled with friends and well-wishers.

Stanley was twenty-two. I was not in love with him. I have never been in love. I married for the sake of having a home.

But now, looking back over my life, how I was called and then trained to develop as the medium I became, it is clear beyond all doubt that Stanley himself was part of the plan. His role was crucial.

His artistic brother Arthur was the apple of his mother's eye and any money the family had was lavished on him. He was trained and set up as an engraver with his own practice, working from home, which gave him freedom to pursue his music. Stanley was the academic one and should have gone to University but his needs never seemed to be taken into account. On our marriage his family provided a small van so that he could start up a one-man haulage business. Unfortunately the van was stolen one night and in the very long delay before he received any compensation from the insurance claim, not only did he have no livelihood but he lost his business clientèle. His father, being a successful butcher found Stanley employment at Smithfield market, work which left his academic ambitions completely unsatisfied. His mental energy, his mind for research, would find their outlet in all kinds of sudden crazes. He would pursue these as far as he could, then, coming up against the hard fact that there was no money for him to study seriously and to follow up any line of research, he would switch to the next thing that caught his fancy. Sadly, he was always something of a square peg in a round hole. At the same time he was a very sensitive man with tremendous kindness, sometimes embarrassingly so. I remember an occasion when he came home from Smithfield wearing canvas shoes. He had given his own stout boots, he told me, to "a poor old man who had nothing".

I was nineteen when our first baby was due, and

Part II: Marriage and Mediumship 37

neither Stanley nor I knew anything about psychic matters.

We had two rooms in a very old house over a shop in Red Lion Square. So old, in fact, that when Stanley removed the plaster in the course of redecorating, the laths were still in the form of branches of trees, so it must have been built before laths were shaped; very old indeed. Our bedroom was quite large, with our bed on one wall. To the right was the window, to the left was the door to the stairs and opposite was the fireplace. Beside the fireplace was a very large cupboard filled with trunks and boxes and all kinds of rarely used things.

Stanley had to be at the meat market in Smithfield at about quarter past five. This meant walking the three miles or so (there was no transport then) and he had to leave our rooms in Red Lion Square at about half past four or quarter to five. Lighting was by gas in those days; one lit a mantle which glowed and either side of the bracket which held it was a chain, one side to increase the flame, the other to lower it or put it out. When Stanley got up he would light the gas and leave it on at a very low level while he ate his breakfast, which I would leave ready for him, then come and say goodbye to me before turning the light out and leaving.

On this occasion I thought I saw him put the light out but after I heard the door close behind him the room was filled with a peculiar yellow light. I was just thinking that he had forgotten to turn the light out when I saw, directly opposite the bed, the door to this walk-in cupboard slowly start to open. Then out came a figure. She did not walk, she seemed to float and in the peculiar light I saw that she was dressed in Plantagenet clothes with the tall head-dress and the filmy draperies of that period. I lay paralysed with fear as she came floating across towards me and up to my side of the bed – the left-hand side which was parallel with the door – when, bending over me, she cursed me with a venom that was as overpowering as it was unexpected. So powerful were the animosity and hate that emanated from her that I broke out in a cold sweat. Then, just as suddenly, the room was in darkness again.

As I lay cold and sick, trying to gather my wits together, the door on my left started to open. I screamed and must have fainted for a moment because the next thing I knew was Stanley kneeling beside the bed and comforting me. When I had recovered sufficiently to tell him what had happened I realised that he must have been well on his way to Smithfield when this figure appeared to me.

'What made you come back?' I asked.

'I heard you calling me. You were shouting for me and I thought something had happened to the baby and I knew I must come home.'

Neither of us realised at the time how extraordinary this was. I had not uttered a word, I had not even thought about him, I was so terrified, so, on looking back, I realise that even in those early days something was being exercised on a psychic level. I never had an experience like that again and because, at that time, we were both so ignorant about these things we just tried our best to forget it. Philip, our son, was born about three weeks later, and I think that in this late stage of my pregnancy my psychic sense was heightened and that there was some kind of psychometrised atmosphere in the room. Something must have happened there that I tuned into accidentally.

Money was extremely short. I had always been a good manager. Even when I was at school it was I who did the meagre shopping we could afford because my mother worked a very long day and by the time she finished the shops would all be shut, except for the fish and chips shop. On Fridays she would be paid and I well remember how, when she came home on Thursday evenings, she would turn out her purse. She would only have pennies left, but whatever it was, I would take it to the fish and chips place and get what I could. If she had three pennies I could buy a twopenny piece of fish and a pennyworth of chips – "tuppence" and "a pennorth" in the language of the time, because they were recognised shopping units. But however carefully I stretched every penny I could not manage on what Stanley earned, especially after our second child, Derek, was born. Philip was two years older. I needed to earn some money but I was quite determined that I would not neglect the children.

Quite near to where we lived the Foundling Hospital in Guildford Street was something of a landmark. I understood it had been founded by Handel because of an abandoned child he took pity on. It was a beautiful building standing well back from the road in large grounds, at the entrance to which was an enormous iron gate. At opposite ends of this gate small marble basins, somewhat like washbasins, were built into the wall, one bearing the word BOYS and the other GIRLS. Beside each basin was a bell and, in the days when foundlings were taken in, anyone leaving a baby would place it in the appropriate basin and ring the bell, when they could slip away unseen, knowing that a nun would come and collect the infant. We used to see the older ones playing on the streets and what interested me was that neither the boys nor the girls ever crossed over. There was nothing to stop them but they never, ever crossed over that pathway. On Sundays you could attend the church there and the boys would be on one side and the girls on another, the girls dressed attractively with little Dutch bonnets and tiny organza aprons over a blue dress, though during the week all the children looked as if they had been dressed in sacks.

Later a day nursery and play school were opened in this building where other children could be cared for from nine in the morning until half past three and I felt I could safely leave Derek and Philip there while I did a part-time job, but I was always there to take them home. I determined they would never come back to an empty home.

In the early days of our marriage Stanley pursued many different interests. After a study of trees he dabbled in phrenology for quite a while and then he became gripped by Egyptology. I went along with these interests in the cause of domestic harmony but during my second pregnancy with Derek I had not enjoyed trailing around the slippery floors of the Egyptian Rooms at the British Museum, my attention focussed on not losing my footing. Strangely enough, it was because of the créche where Derek and Philip were looked after that my gradual – and, it must be said, extremely reluctant – introduction to mediumship began.

I took an active part in any social life I could get and attended weekly meetings of the mothers at the Foundling Hospital with enthusiasm. In the evening people would come and talk to us on all kinds of subjects. We had dressmaking competitions and we formed a choir. I greatly enjoyed this relaxation away from domesticity and I was elected to the committee responsible for arranging the entertainment for these social evenings. Seeking new ideas, I asked Stanley if he could find a book in the library that might offer some promising suggestions. He brought home a book on parlour games and what caught my eye was a section on table tilting. On reading the first paragraph, not more than half a page, immediately his interest was aroused, and because it was much easier to go along with his various interests, I agreed to try. Stanley carefully followed the instructions in the book; you had to have a small table, you recited the alphabet, and when the table stopped moving, that would be the letter.

We used a Victorian table and spelled out the letters as instructed. Or, rather, Stanley had an exercise book and with one free hand to write down the letters placed the other on the table, along with both of my hands, our fingers touching. A most extraordinary sensation followed. It was as if the table became fluid, as if it was pulsating. It was not solid at all, it was like a piece of cloth with air beneath it. This movement started immediately we put our hands and fingers together on the table and it became so rapid in its dictation that Stanley had no time at all to separate the words or know what they were. He just wrote down letter after letter after letter in this children's exercise book. We filled about six pages. It was intensely tiring and very tedious but the table was in no doubt about its movements at all. Then, just as suddenly as it had begun, it stopped dead and the thing was a solid table again.

It took a long time to separate out the words. Another curious feature was that they were all spelt phonetically.

However, at last, when Stanley had laboriously deciphered all this we found we had been given pages and pages of information purporting to come from my father and relating to my parents' three short years of marriage in Middlesbrough. As I was only three months old when my father died I could not verify any of it so we waited to show it to my mother the next evening. She was astonished. The information included such facts as who their neighbours had been and details about my father's work. My mother confirmed that it was entirely accurate, including much that she had forgotten until it was recalled by this communication.

Needless to say we were deeply impressed with this and Stanley became avid to try again. We did so many times but although the table pulsated and gave us letters, these formed no words, they were nonsense. With hindsight, we recognised that the first occasion had fulfilled its purpose of ensuring Stanley's irrevocable interest. No more flitting from one subject to another, now he began to read seriously about survival and communication. Oliver Lodge, Conan Doyle, Stainton Moses – all their books now came into our home. Stanley read a lot about spirit cooperation, about their help if we made ourselves available. My mother shrugged her shoulders.

'At least it's a change from hieroglyphics,' she said.

'Maybe,' I retorted with feeling, 'but it's wasting an awful lot of my time.'

Then, on one of these occasions, the table told us that a cousin of mine who used sometimes to visit us had met with an accident and that Stanley should go to her as she needed help. I have forgotten now where she was supposed to be but

Stanley went as directed and the message proved to be entirely false. This experience overlaid the quite astounding accuracy of our first experiment with the table. I have since learned that such false messages are often part of early psychic experimentation, whether designed to emphasise the need for caution and common sense in this field, as in any other, I do not know. Perhaps the object was to turn us away from this method and to seek further, because Stanley had discovered that there were places where one could receive messages from the spirit world (he never called them churches) and this is what he embarked on next. Getting my mother to babysit, we went to a place in Tottenham Court Road.

I was twenty-one then and Stanley four years older but we both looked extremely young. With my jet-black, shining hair (I was very proud of my hair) cut in a Japanese style with a fringe, I looked about fourteen. We took our places somewhat hesitantly at the end of a row, Stanley, six feet tall with very long legs, sat uncomfortably in the cramped space with his legs sticking out into the aisle. We can hardly have looked like a married couple but to our astonishment the medium, looking at me, said,

'I want to come to your husband, the gentleman sitting at the end of the row.'

I tried to shrink down behind the row in front. Turning now to Stanley, the medium went on:

'You are sitting with a table.'

Stanley nearly fell off his chair with astonishment, but he nodded and she continued to address him.

'You are sitting with your wife.'

Stanley nodded.

'She is a potential medium. She is very gifted. Forget about the table and sit together. You'll be surprised at the results.'

Hearing this my heart sank. I had hoped this was another of Stanley's passing enthusiasms because, although we were getting no results with the table, he would insist on trying and it was taking up far too much of my time. In retrospect, I suppose I should be grateful she did not tell him to dip me in the river because I am sure he would have done whatever she said. He came home highly elated. Although he had read a bit about sitting for development, he had very little to go on as regards the actual procedure. After this message he decided it would be better if we sat in the cupboard because he had read about the conservation of power in a small space. He cleared the cupboard except for one very large trunk which did duty as a seat and, he said, we would sit in the dark.

Stanley insisted that it had to be in the dark. He had read Sir Arthur Conan Doyle's account of what he received through his wife's mediumship; how he used to sit opposite her and she would go into trance, when her guide would speak to him. With his usual fanaticism, Stanley insisted we must sit every night. I had two infants to take care of, Philip about three and Derek still a baby, and after they were in bed I needed that time to catch up with all the work I could not get done during the day. This latest fad of Stanley's was getting to be too much for me. Certainly, I was not in the right state of mind for sitting in a cupboard in the dark, evening after evening, while nothing happened.

In the years to come I could see that Stanley was very much more sensitive and psychically aware than either of us realised because, at that early stage, neither of us even knew what such things meant. I think he must have received inner guidance to persevere with what we were doing because for weeks we sat, in darkness, every night, with nothing to give us any encouragement. My mind would be racing around all the things I could usefully be doing during this time which, to me, was completely wasted. It was hardly surprising that I was in a state of rebellion, which reached a climax about six weeks later. We had been sitting for forty minutes, which is an extremely long time in the dark with nothing whatever happening, when I said to myself,

'I don't care if it means divorce, I am *not* doing this any more.'

I did not say it aloud, it was in my mind, and suddenly I was holding two sticks in my hands. They were quite solid, I can almost feel them now, a slight roughness in the wood, they were not polished, and I felt myself beating a drum with a rhythm that seemed to move my hands of its own accord. I found myself saying, 'Drums! Drums!' out loud, and then it all vanished.

Stanley and I nearly fell off the trunk.

'What happened to you?' he demanded eagerly.

'I don't know. I was just beating a drum.'

'Right,' he said, 'we are going back to one of those places to see if we can find out more.'

This time we went to a different Spiritualist church and the medium had never seen us before. She came directly to me and said,

'I don't have a message for you from your spirit friends but I am being impressed that it is important I say "drums" to you, and I want to say also that you are holding the drumsticks in your hands.'

Stanley and I were astounded. This did not help us at all by way of explanation but it satisfied Stanley that we were right to persevere and it stimulated him to explore further.

But why "drums" we naturally wondered? I knew that my father had been in the army but until I asked my mother I had no idea of any connection with drums. She told me that he had been a drummer boy, I think it was when he went to India and to Aden with the regiment. There was a very curious sequel to this many, many years afterwards. Late in my life, long after Stanley had died, through my professional work I met an elderly, somewhat eccentric and certainly lonely lady who seemed to find something in me which she needed, because she was very persistent in pursuing the contact. It was not my mediumship that interested her, what she sought was more personal. I must have mentioned my father, that, as a boy, he had been in the army, because she wrote me in great excitement about a book she had just read, in which the author contrasted the insignificant rank of the drummer with the importance of his role in marching out in front. This author actually mentioned my father by name, George Henry Fitzpatrick, in front with his drum on some notable occasion.

I thought this quite extraordinary; it made a kind of link between us which she had always so much wanted. In another way, in retrospect, I can see its significance as a symbol: the drummer leads and those behind follow. Under Chan's guidance I have always pioneered my own method of mediumship and later, under Chan's direction, when my training of mediums became such a major part of my work, I have always taught his pioneering methods. That, however, was very far into the future.

What this episode did was to rekindle my interest. Stanley, meanwhile, had learned a bit more sense and we spaced out our times for sitting to once or twice a week. I went along with this rather less reluctantly now, wondering if something else would happen. By this time we had three rooms, on the second and top floors of the same house, and we no longer sat in the cupboard but in the sitting room.

Stanley and I were together one evening after the children were in bed. This was after the medium had told us we did not need a table but we still sat in the dark. There we were, waiting, my interest pretty low, when a note was struck on the piano. Stanley was thrilled.

'If that is you, friend,' he said, 'will you please strike a note again?'

The note was struck again, just one note, then there was a pause.

'Is it all right if I put the light on?' asked Stanley.

Again one note was struck.

I have described the gas lighting of those days, a mantle with a chain each side, one controlling the pilot light for the mantle. Very gently Stanley pulled and slowly the light came on. Turning my head, I saw our enormous tabby cat with his paw lifted above the keys poised for the next note. After being secretly rather frightened I was now almost hysterical with laughter. Stanley was furious.

CHAPTER 5

Reluctantly sitting in the dark. Chan enters their lives. Stanley embarks on a protracted experiment to prove survival. Near-fatal illness of their elder son. They adopt a baby girl.

It is interesting in retrospect to note how very apathetic I was about my development. Stanley had read how Sir Arthur Conan Doyle used to sit with his wife and through her mediumship a great many communications were given to him. This became Stanley's goal and the model for how we would sit very regularly together in the dark. When I recapture my thoughts from those days I realise it was Stanley's overriding enthusiasm which carried us along until we reached our next encouragement. This happened just as suddenly as the drum episode. Impossible to describe, but it was as if I stepped behind myself and something came in front of me. I was fully conscious but with no control over my speech. It was as if something was *making* me speak.

That was how Chan entered into our lives, with a few intermittent words spoken through me which I allowed because I had no idea what was happening or what I should do. Of course it was a very long time before our partnership built up and Chan told me later that this passive acquiescence on my part enabled him to take control and guide and discipline my natural gift. Chan told Stanley that if he would play his part by continuing to sit regularly with me, he would provide the instruction for the training of my mediumship. From that point my tuition began in a serious way.

He asked Stanley to take notes, which he did, copiously. We had endless exercise books with his instructions in those early days which, to my very great regret, I did not keep. Week by week, month by month, Chan gave specific directions for my training, though I had no idea that this would lead to my becoming a medium. Nor would I have accepted this at the time but it was easier to go along with Stanley than to object.

I do remember being impressed that spirit friends could be attracted to oneself and wanting very much to attract Dame Nellie Melba to me. Naive as I was in deceiving myself, I thought that if I sat by myself she would come. I did not say anything to Stanley for fear of being laughed at but while the children were at nursery school one afternoon I went into the sitting room and tried mentally to link with her. I even changed my dress. Of course nothing happened. Years later, when I was ready, I tried again alone to prove something to myself and then I succeeded.

It is difficult for me now to recall the course of Chan's early tuition but it proceeded steadily as he had promised. He did not confine it to what I later came to call the mechanics of mediumship but skilfully enlarged on what he taught me, constantly introducing some fresh aspect or other; how I should use my voice to avoid strain, for instance. Here my love of singing was a great help because, although I had never had any formal tuition, through books I had tried to learn how to breathe properly. As I came to realise later – many, many years later – there is a very close analogy between learning the full register of one's voice and how to control it through right breathing, and learning the range and control of the psychic centres in mediumship. He taught me diction. If I mispronounced a word he would not correct me but it was rather like singing a note out of tune. I would somehow feel uneasy.

I was now very much more conscious of what was being said but I did not remember it and it was still necessary for Stanley to take notes and to verify things afterwards. During this stage it often seemed to me as if another person was present and that it was to that other person that I was listening but I could not retain it. Chan explained that I was receiving the tuition on a different level of consciousness and that it would be absorbed into my subconscious mind, ready to be recalled when needed, but that I would not remember it as a conscious process of learning. As aspects of my training proceeded according to my level of understanding, each became part of a whole which I was gradually taking in.

And so we continued, step by step. For instance, in due course, deportment:

'Don't stand still,' Chan would say. 'Move about, move your hands and your head. Turn to face the people in different places.'

This seemed to me a bit ludicrous at the time because in trance I had no idea of what was going on with my head or my hands. Later, however, when I worked on the platform in my normal consciousness, this training surfaced and proved invaluable. Chan insisted I should always try to make myself look as nice as possible, then forget entirely about my appearance, stressing that if I was worrying about that I would be of no use to them. They had to get *me* out of the way.

Another curious paradox was only explained to me in years to come when my partnership with Chan was well established. Stanley was always a great reader and when he turned this interest to psychical matters Chan was able to make use of his knowledge. I, on the other hand, since my schooldays, had hardly read at all, completely occupied as I was with the children and my domestic and part-time work. This relatively blank and fluid state of my mind at that time enabled Chan to exercise his influence on me right from the beginning without having to overcome any rigid thoughts or set ideas. The paradox was that in a later phase, when I was starting to become a useful instrument for his communication, he encouraged me to read widely again in order to stock my mind. Chan has told me that for him my brain is like a typewriter. If the words are there, he can use them. If they are there wrongly, he cannot alter them, I have to do that. He could not tell me the correct way to say a word, but by letting me know it was incorrect I would be prompted to look it up; and by doing that I retained it consciously in my brain.

None of this was revealed to me at the time but when I look back I marvel at the patience, the love, the sincerity of his training; his gentle persistence in introducing what he wanted to convey. In due course, when Chan thought I was ready, he told Stanley to invite other people to sit with us. After that Stanley would bring home two or three from among those he met at Smithfield, different sitters each week, so that Chan could practise with me on someone about whom I knew absolutely nothing.

At this early stage, however, I was a puppet. Furthermore, at that time Chan did not really mean much to me. I had to accept him because he had, as it were, become a member of our family. Even the children, who were growing up a bit now, regarded him as part of their family too, because Stanley's conversation during these years revolved around what Chan had said or done.

We still went to services from time to time for verification of what Chan had said the previous night and sometimes we received surprising messages. One stays in my mind very clearly. The medium came to us and said, 'You have a little boy.' To our astonishment she then proceeded to tell us that this little boy had learned to climb onto a stool from which he managed to open a window, when he would perch there and look out. She had been impressed to give us this warning.

The children's room was on the second floor. Clearly if this was true it was very dangerous. I knew it was not Philip, Derek was always the adventurous one. As we never left them alone at home, this must be taking place while we or my mother, in another room, thought they were safely playing in theirs. Next morning I asked Derek,

'Can you open the window?'

'Sometimes,' he said.

'Well,' I explained, 'I have had a message from Chan about it. He had to tell me because it is dangerous, you could hurt yourself very badly and Chan says you must never do it again.'

This impressed Derek. By now both children accepted Chan as our family mentor. Perhaps it was unusual but it seemed completely natural to us all at the time.

Stanley had convinced himself of the reality of survival. Before accepting it he had of course embarked on a study of all that he could lay his hands on; what most impressed him was the weakness of the arguments against and, with his passion for research, he longed to produce positive proof. Finally, after a great deal of thought, he decided there was only one proof which would eliminate all possibility of telepathic or emotional interference. This would be to receive evidence from someone about whom we knew absolutely nothing, who, through me, would communicate their identity together with a body of background material, the accuracy of which he could subsequently confirm or disprove.

At our next sitting he asked Chan if an experiment along those lines would be possible. This was a considerable time after the early years of our contact with Chan; we were now receiving specific instructions which Stanley would faithfully carry out. Yes, agreed Chan, but it would take a long time. It would be like a jig-saw puzzle and Stanley would have to be very persevering and very patient. Chan, through me, would provide the various bits of evidence for Stanley to record and, lastly, at the end of the experiment, he would disclose the location where the accuracy of the information could be proved.

And so they embarked on this undertaking. (I still tended to think of "they". The event which was to reverse this outlook and lead to my total commitment was a little way ahead.)

Chan started by telling us of a young lady whom he referred to as Kathleen and week by week he would add some little detail. Kathleen, he said, belonged to a family who had lived for several generations in the same area. He mentioned sons and daughters to Stanley and told him that there were two or three doctors in this family. He gave us the names – Christian names only, and these at different times – of the family.

In due course, we learned that Kathleen, her parents and various other relatives were buried in the same churchyard. A very specific piece of information was that one member of the family died in Newmarket. He was a doctor and he was commemorated at the family grave in the churchyard but his body was actually buried at Newmarket. Along with basic facts he gave various details and odd items that were quite useless in themselves. Stanley, meticulous in his note-taking, recorded all this information as it came through me.

These snippets were not given in any systematic way. Chan would be talking about something quite different and suddenly would interpose,

'About this other matter,' and quickly give further detail.

He did this, he explained, because at that time my trance was relatively light and he wanted to ensure that my mind took no part in the experiment. In fact, I was still indifferent to this part of what we were doing, it did not strike me as particularly significant.

Stanley collected information week by week over a period of nine months in this fragmented way. He had the parents, he had the children, he had various brothers and sisters. He also had a description of the churchyard in which they were buried; not a cemetery, a graveyard attached to a church. When Stanley had gradually received all this information after these nine months of painstaking notes, Chan said,

'Now I will give you the name of the family.'

(If my memory is correct, it was Collins). The other fact he now disclosed was the location of the family grave: in the village churchyard in Farlingham in Kent. He told Stanley to go there with his book of facts and tick off, one by one, the various details which he had been able to convey through my mediumship.

Stanley, full of his usual enthusiasm and elated at this prospect, could hardly wait until Sunday. We used often to go out on our bicycles on Sundays while my mother looked after the children. We were living in Leytonstone then and would normally ride into the Essex countryside with a picnic. It was a very long way indeed from Leytonstone to Farlingham in Kent but we had no money for transport so we had no choice but to go there on our bicycles. This involved cycling over cobblestones and rough-surfaced roads from East Essex, where we lived, into Kent, through the miles of congested streets which make up outer London. It was a hard, unpleasant ride, our only refreshment what we took with us, we could not afford to buy anything along the way. It must have taken us three or four hours each way but Stanley's satisfaction made up for our almost physical collapse by the time we got home again.

To his great delight he was able to verify, fact by fact, all that he had been told. We found the graves just as they had been described, some surrounded by a square of railings, others simple graves with a tombstone. We found Kathleen's grandfather with the original name. We found the uncles and aunts with their married names and were able to verify the details we had been given about the locations of the various graves.

Most striking of all, we found confirmation that one member of the family, a doctor as we had been told, had indeed died in Newmarket and was actually buried there, a fact engraved on his memorial; a white, newer-looking stone in contrast to the older, grey appearance of the others – again, just as we had been told. Stanley took a photograph of this and of another imposing tomb surrounded by a railing. His tenacity in following up the numerous clues, which themselves had entailed a good deal of effort from the spirit world, was richly rewarded and, for his part, we were now really launched on this path, though I was still quite lukewarm about it.

It may seem difficult to understand now why we made no attempt to interest anyone formally in this evidence or to have it recorded, but Stanley had no use for psychical research organisations because of what he considered their negative bias and it would never have occurred to me at this time.

That the spirit world can also work powerfully in helpful and very unexpected ways was brought home to us by a sudden illness of our son Philip, eight or nine years old when he complained of tummy pains one Friday. The family doctor, who knew us all quite well, was reassuring, brushing the pain away as just a tummy upset. On Saturday Philip still complained of the pain but he went out to play, though looking very white. On the Sunday he was obviously worse and seemed very distressed. Having consulted the doctor on Friday and knowing how up and down children can be, I was not unduly worried. However, I felt sure there would be a message for me from our spirit friends if we had reason to be concerned – we had come to rely on this source of information – so on Sunday evening I went to the Spiritualist Church in Stratford, two or three miles away. I received nothing from the platform and went home somewhat reassured.

By Monday morning Philip was seriously ill, his stomach was like a board. We sent for the doctor who rushed him to hospital where the surgeon said Philip had a ruptured appendix. He did not know whether he could save him but he would try. I was simply staggered. I felt terribly let down and disappointed. After the operation we were told that they could not offer any real hope that Philip would survive and it would be best if Stanley and I stayed until morning.

Stanley, however, refused to do this.

'We believe in spiritual healing,' he said to me. 'I believe I can do my son more good if we go away and pray for him in his own home.'

I was so distressed and worried, I was anxious to stay with Philip, but Stanley overrode my objections. I remember weeping uncontrollably on the tram going home and people staring at me. My mother was at home, she had stayed with Derek. Stanley broke the news to her and then we each tried to concentrate on sending healing. While we were sitting quietly in this way someone came to the door. One of our regular sitters was standing there sheepishly to tell us that at church the previous evening he had been asked if he knew of a little boy called Philip, and when he said he did, was told that the child was very, very ill. When our sitter had last seen Philip only days ago he was running around happily, so he answered,

'Not as far as I know.'

'Oh, yes he is,' said the medium, 'but he is going to be all right. Tell his mother he will pull through.'

This amazed us but about half an hour later there was another ring at the door. A student, one of our sitters, had been to a completely different church and received a message to the same effect.

'Do you know anyone called Philip? He is extremely ill.'

'No,' the student replied, 'he is quite well.'

'Oh, no, he's not,' said the medium, 'but tell his parents that they did the right thing and he is going to recover.'

These messages, coming from two totally different sources in such a remarkable way, were reassuring, although I was afraid to believe them. Unable to contain my anxiety, at five o'clock next morning I set out. The hospital was about three miles away and there was no transport. I had to walk.

It was a beautiful May morning and I can remember, when I arrived, walking through the hospital grounds past a glorious bank of colour and scent, golden wallflowers and contrasting pink tulips. I breathed in the vitality that comes from such massed flowers even as I braced myself for what I was going to find.

Philip, as a boy, had the most exquisite colouring; he had purple eyes with those smutty finger smudges under them and very dark hair. I felt my heart turn over when I saw him sitting propped up in bed. The nurse who led me in said,

'I don't know how he survived. It's a miracle. The surgeon, everyone, gave him up. They said it was hopeless.'

I had eyes only for Philip but I heard her add,

'He's still very weak, you musn't stay long, but he is going to be all right.'

'Oh, Philip,' I said ' I'm *so* glad you're better. I didn't realise how ill you were. I'm so sorry.'

'That's all right, Mummy,' he said, 'but I wouldn't have minded – you know – going away. I went somewhere, and it was very nice.'

I was comforted afterwards that he had had no fear and that he had understood this brief experience of the spirit world, but what I could not understand was why the reassuring communications had come through other mediums to two separate people and not directly to Stanley and me. At the next opportunity we asked Chan why, when I had gone on the Sunday night in the hope of receiving a message, they had not given one.

'Had we reassured you then,' he said, 'you might have delayed next morning. Half an hour longer would have been too late.'

This was exactly what the surgeon had told us, that if we had left it any longer they could not even have attempted to save Philip.

It had been very much against my own wishes that Stanley insisted we did not stay by his bed all night but that we should go home and pray with total concentration. Thinking about this afterwards I felt that, without realising it, Stanley must have been impressed to do this by Chan and our spirit helpers. This whole experience was another lesson to me, one with wide implications, and another step in my understanding of spiritual companionship and support.

We now had our two much-loved sons. I had made up my mind when Derek was born that we would not have any more children, but Stanley and I both dearly wanted a little girl. When Derek was about six we decided to adopt one. Adoption was very different in those days. We wrote to the Salvation Army and were given an appointment at their Mothers' Hospital in Clapton. The authorities there did not approve of adoption, believing that mothers should retain their responsibility for their children even if illegitimate. Fostering was what they favoured but although we were accepted as suitable foster parents it was a long time before they were able to offer us a baby girl.

However, in due course we received notification that a baby girl was available for fostering. When we arrived at the appointment we did not meet the mother; only the baby was brought in. She was completely bald with a dead white face. It gave me a shock when I saw her. We learned afterwards that she had never been outside the building in the whole of her six months. It was explained to us that any arrangements would have to be finalised with the mother but first of all they needed to know whether we were willing to take this baby. Extremely disappointed though we both were, and somewhat reluctantly, we agreed. As we left I said to Stanley, 'She looks like one of those Sally Lunns from the bakery, that pale, round face with no hair.' From that moment she was always Sally to us, although her real name was Christine. About three weeks later I brought her home.

It was one of their regulations that the mother must visit her baby at the foster home each week and pay ten shillings weekly towards the child's keep. I was quite willing to take her for nothing but the rule was strict. As a foster parent I had to register with the Child Welfare Association who sent a representative to inspect our home. We had a pleasant little house then, very unpretentious but with three bedrooms and a small garden. Quite a young woman came and from her visit we became good friends. When she was in the neighbourhood she would often come in unofficially for a cup of tea and a chat.

All we knew about Sally's mother – whom I will call Dolly – was that her family lived in Lowestoft and that she had been sent to London when they discovered she was pregnant. Now for the first time we met her. She was working at the Mothers' Hospital and living in. On her weekly half-day she came quite regularly to see Sally and although she seemed to get on quite well with me and my mother we never learned any more about her or anything of her own personal life. Conversationally she was like a deaf mute. I offered not to take her ten shillings a week but Dolly insisted. I felt rather guilty about taking money for a little girl I had wanted so much, so, although money was still very tight, I tried to put this on one side and buy something special for Sally. The boys thought her a bit of a joke and they quite enjoyed having her in the family. There were very few times in my married life when I was not doing an outside job of some kind to earn a little money, but this happened to be one of them and it was a very happy time.

My mother was living with us and, somewhat to my surprise, she and Sally took to each other immediately. They became devoted to each other, which was very good for me, especially when I started to become known professionally and she took over more and more of my domestic responsibilities.

Ivy with her brother outside their first London home.

Ivy as a schoolgirl.

Growing up.

Ivy's mother and her brother Harry.

Above: Stanley, in a production of "Ruddigore", June 1924.

Left: Ivy and Stanley on their wedding day in 1927.
Below: Ivy and Stanley shortly after their marriage.

Stanley in "H.M.S. Pinafore", May 1924.

Stanley soon after marriage..

Ivy in Brighton with her hostess who soon became a good friend.

Below left: Ivy's brother Harry.
Below right: Ivy. A birthday

Above and left: Farningham Churchyard. The proof!

Right: Stanley with Philip.

Below: Ivy and Stanley.

Ivy's sons, Derek (left) and Philip.

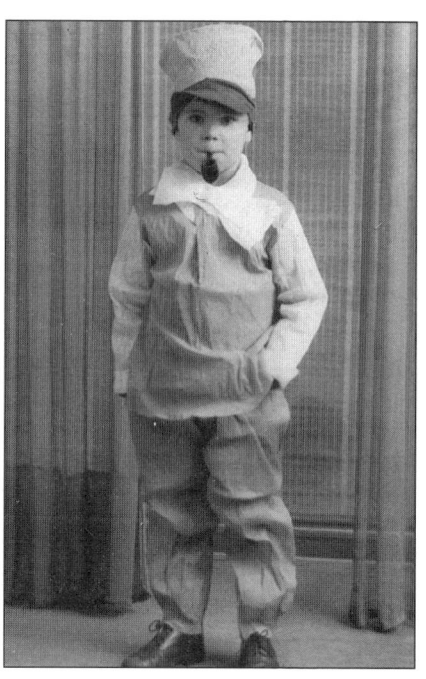

Derek in fancy dress.

Philip.

Ivy in 1975. "The complete professional".

Ivy is dumbfounded when the chairman announces she is "The Spiritualist of 1971". Guests at her table — she had a party of 60 — applaud the decision.

Ivy in the 1980s.

Psychic portrait of Ivy's spirit guide "CHAN" by Carol Polge.

Janet and Ivy at a birthday celebration at the London Spiritual Mission, Pembridge Place, in 1984.

CHAPTER 6

A demonstration by Estelle Roberts changes Ivy's indifference to genuine dedication. Her training intensified. First appearance on a platform. Is Chan real, she wonders?

In due course Stanley's enthusiasm began to cool. He had satisfied himself that it was possible to get accurate communication – that piece of research had been successfully completed – and while he remained interested in my own development, neither of us believed that it would ever amount to much. For my part, I still feared that my own mind interfered a great deal with the communications. In order to eliminate this suspicion of self-suggestion, part of Chan's training of me at this time was to direct us to various Spiritualist churches where, through different mediums, he would provide verification of what I had received in our own small home circle. Stanley was now quite content for my mother to accompany me on these occasions while he stayed at home with the children.

By this time we knew a number of centres we could attend for any verification needed and Chan would periodically direct us to a particular church on a particular day. I suppose he chose them because of the medium who would be there, knowing that he could get the information through that particular medium. It was not always his exact words repeated but during the seven or eight years of my training I never knew him to fail me when he had promised verification at a particular church; not literally, but the sense of what he had communicated.

On one of these occasions, after verifying something that Chan had told us, the medium went on to say,

'And your guide is also telling me that you will witness every form of mediumship – direct voice, transfiguration, materialisation – all these you will witness because it is important for you to be able to stand on a platform and declare the truth of these things from your own experience.'

At the time this seemed ludicrous. I could not imagine myself on a platform and we had no money for any extras. I knew one could attend such demonstrations but the cost ruled them out entirely for us. Nevertheless, this promise also was fulfilled. In due course I did indeed witness all these things and it never cost me a farthing.

When Chan told me I should go and hear Estelle Roberts – the foremost medium of that day – and see exactly how she demonstrated, it proved to be a watershed for me. What is now the Spiritualist Association of Great Britain was then the Marylebone Spiritualist Association based in Bloomsbury and they used to hire a large hall in Southampton Row. On Sundays, coming home from a walk with the children we used to see crowds queueing outside the entrance. Occasionally we would see Estelle Roberts arriving, a distinguished figure in the beautiful velvet cloak that she always wore.

At the time Chan told me to go and watch her demonstration she had left the Marylebone Spiritualist Association and was working independently. She had taken the Odeon Hall in Bond Street above Chappells, the piano people, a very beautiful room, reached by a side door from a flight of steps that by-passed the shop. My mother and I arrived early, knowing that for an Estelle Roberts demonstration one might not otherwise get in. The stairs were carpeted and we had sat down on an upper step to wait for the doors to open when we were joined by a very ordinary-looking woman in a navy blue costume with a very large hat. Sitting on the step immediately below us she looked up timidly and asked, very hesitantly, if we had been there before. I replied that we had not seen Mrs Roberts demonstrate but that we knew of her and about what she did.

As this lady then told us that her brother, a vicar, had just died, she burst into tears. 'I'm so ashamed,' she said. 'Here I am, the sister of a vicar. I have supported him all these years and now that he has died I have no belief, no comfort. I have nothing I can hold onto, and I am so ashamed.' Here she wiped some fresh tears away and murmured as if to herself, 'If only he could tell me that he is still around *somewhere*! Then I feel I could face life without him.'

She went on to tell us that he had only suffered a brief illness. It was still the custom then to bring the dead home and the night before he was to be buried she had entered the room where his coffin was placed in the centre. She went up to the open coffin, took hold of his hand and held it, and said, "Oh, Charles, if there is anything – anything at all – that you can tell me that will assure me that you have not gone, please, please, try!"

'Then,' she told us, 'for some reason I went across the room to where I had put a vase of roses. I took one, I snapped off the stem and I uncurled his fingers and placed it between his fingers and the palm of his hand, and closed them again.' She went on: 'I don't know how I heard of this lady but somehow her name was given to me, and the address of this place. I don't really know why I am here, it may be very wicked of me, but I must know. I must know one way or the other.'

My mother and I felt terribly sorry for this woman. Our hearts went out to her and when the doors opened she came in and sat beside us. In due course Estelle Roberts entered, her appearance and her somewhat regal bearing just as I had observed from the street when passing by. After greeting the audience she launched confidently into her demonstration giving message after message that, judging from the way in which they were received, were remarkable in the accuracy of their detail. This went on until nearly the end, when she said,

'I want to come to the lady sitting near the back. The lady in navy with a very large hat.'

I nudged her and told her just to answer "Yes". She lifted her head and murmured assent.

'Your brother is here,' announced Estelle Roberts from the platform. 'He has asked me to say that he heard exactly what you were asking of him and that yes, of course he is still with you and of course he will continue in his love and protection of you. He is telling me that you did this -' and she turned and marched across the platform to a vase of flowers, took one out and snapped the stem. 'You brought it back,' she went on, 'You uncurled his hand, you placed the flower within his fingers and you put it back on his chest. He knew,' she said. 'He is saying "I knew. I was there and I will always be there."'

That was the last message of the afternoon.

The lady's tears after that were of joy and for the very first time I realised what a wonderful gift mediumship could be. As we walked slowly down the stairs I thought, 'If that is what it's all about; if I can give that comfort to someone in bereavement, then I am going to be a medium.' It really mattered to me. Perhaps not quite a St Paul's conversion but this was the turning point, the beginning of my real dedication, quite different from the times when Stanley had made promises on my behalf.

From time to time during the years of my tuition Chan would ask if we were ready to make this work our priority. Stanley always promised, I did not have any say in the matter then. He would tell me afterwards, saying our spirit friends needed to know if we were going to continue this work alongside ordinary life, or if we were going to make it a priority.

'You might have asked me,' I would say, but without attaching a great deal of importance to the matter.

It was only now, following this Estelle Roberts demonstration, that I agreed to make this work my priority.

'You do realise,' said Chan at our next sitting, 'that this is now going to demand certain sacrifices in your life?'

'What sacrifices?' asked Stanley.

When Chan told us that this work would interfere with our domestic life, that it would take precedence over our social life and over other arrangements we might have made, Stanley brushed this aside, explaining that we had hardly any social commitments. This was true, largely because we could not afford them. Now Chan needed my confirmation and Stanley told me that he made a great deal about what our promise would mean. I gave my promise, not foreseeing any problem. Another promise extracted from us at this time of my dedication was that, in no circumstances would I ask for an engagement. The possibility that anyone would ever want to engage me seemed so remote that without hesitation we both replied, 'Of course we promise that.'

I was later to learn that it was quite customary for mediums, especially in the early days when they were not well known, to take their engagement diaries with them and ask for future engagements. But I can say that I have never broken that promise, in spite of the fact that there was at least one time when holding to it cost me dear.

We had been sitting for about eight years while Chan had undertaken my tuition. For our regular practice sessions Stanley would find fresh people who were interested, strangers who came only once, and around this time one of these turned up with his lady friend. Towards the end of the session she said to Chan,

'Monday is a very important day for me. I am hoping for a message on Sunday. Will I get one?'

After a slight pause Chan replied,

'Yes, you will get your message. She is a very good medium.'

'I'm sorry,' objected this lady, 'but this can't be. The medium we are expecting on Sunday is a man and he has been booked for a very long time.'

'No,' insisted Chan, 'it is a lady. And you will get your message.'

By now I had learned how a medium can interfere with the accuracy of a message through her own thoughts or prejudices and when Stanley told me about this afterwards, that the lady had clearly been disbelieving, I felt sure it was my fault.

'I reckon I interfered with that,' I said. 'I expected it to be a woman because they nearly always are.'

'Well, there's only one way to find out,' said Stanley, always practical. 'Go along and see for yourself. Do you know where it is?'

I did not but Stanley enquired from the man in the market and learned that the church was in Walthamstow, about four or five miles from where we lived in Leytonstone. By now he had become bored with attending Sunday services himself but, as always, he was very willing to help me in anything connected with my development. Realising that it might well be quite a difficult journey for us, he went there on his bicycle on the Friday evening so that he could tell us how to find it. He told us which bus to take to Walthamstow High Street, after which we had to walk through two or three turnings to reach this rather obscure little church quite some way from the bus stop.

On the Sunday evening my mother and I set out. The church was difficult to find, hidden among the back streets with no sign or direction, so, although we had plenty of time, it was on the dot of half past six when we arrived. My mother's feet troubled her so she had lagged behind while I had gone a little ahead, hoping to get seats for us both. There were three steps up to the entrance and, to my surprise, standing on the top step I saw the lady who had been at our practice session on the Wednesday evening, obviously in a state of anxiety. She grabbed my arm.

'Never say prayers are not answered!' she exclaimed. 'We

have a speaker but no clairvoyant. Come with me.' And she hurried me through and onto the platform. I was so dumbfounded I did not have the wit to refuse.

My mother, meanwhile, had come in and said to the steward on the door,

'Where is she going?'

'Oh,' he replied, 'she's the medium.' My mother nearly collapsed on a chair.

I remember sitting up on the platform paralysed with fear. I was of course familiar with the procedure and I sat numbly through the opening prayer and the address. Then it came to the hymn before the clairvoyance. I did not know what I was going to do. All my training had been in trance, with Chan, but I had never seen anybody at the various churches we visited give clairvoyance in trance from the platform. I was desperate and on the point of thinking I would have to get up and say "I am sorry friends, I can't do this." At that moment I became aware of the familiar cloaking.

It is very peculiar, the way Chan comes. It is as if he pulls an invisible hood over my head. As he does so, the conscious part of me seems to step behind it and he wears the hood. Now this beloved sensation came to my rescue and I heard inside my head: 'Just get out of the way and let me do this.' It seemed to me then as if *he* was up on his feet, giving the messages. I was quite unaware of their content. Afterwards, before the meeting closed, the chairwoman from the platform said how remarkable the clairvoyance had been. It was the lady who had been at our house and she went on to describe what Chan had said on that occasion and how she had thought it must have been the medium's error.

For me it was a wonderful experience. I could not come back to earth for a while, I was like somebody drunk.

When I had recovered from my euphoria I took the first opportunity of asking Chan why he had not told me. 'Would you have gone?' he replied drily. I had to confess I would not. I doubt very much whether he could have overcome my fear if I had known. His hold in those days was considerably less than it became later on, even though he was totally in control with regard to his instruction. It would never have occurred to me to question that, because I, of myself, knew nothing of what I was doing.

Arising from that evening I was invited back to Walthamstow, though it was all of six months before I was offered what I could call a regular engagement, after that first occasion when I was catapulted onto the platform. That was in October 1938. Within a year war had been declared.

Meanwhile, I had my local church in Stratford, not very far from where we lived. I knew I needed more practice but as I could only work in trance, I could not participate, I could only watch and listen. At our weekly sessions at home Chan would take me through anything that had occurred at these services or at the open development circles, and tell me what was good about them – or the reverse.

I was keen to improve, I wanted to be a good medium, and I think it was around this time that I recognised the importance of truly believing. Most of my conviction had come vicariously through Stanley, from what he had discovered and proved for himself. Now I asked myself, do *I* really believe? By this time I was able to converse fairly freely with Chan. He had been teaching me about such things as deportment, presentation, telling me where to go and hear a particular medium or suggesting other particular things I should do. A great deal of his tuition was now on the direct mental level which I was beginning to trust very much more.

Now with my greater sense of seriousness, I wanted very much more to be sure about what I was *really* doing, and I remember saying to Chan that it was very important to me that I should know with certainty that my spirit was separate from my body. How could I prove this for myself? Chan told me that I would have to learn how to detach my spirit, that I must take time in the afternoons when Stanley was at work and the children were at nursery school and I could be quite sure of being undisturbed. I was to lie flat on my bed and will myself, as it were, to rise above my body; to think of myself as elevating.

It took a good many concentrated efforts in this way before I achieved any degree of separation, but by persevering steadily, afternoon after afternoon, I was able gradually to develop this ability until I succeeded in rising higher and higher above my body, though still lying horizontal. I had not yet been able to separate in a standing-up position. Our house was an old one with quite high ceilings and when at last I managed to get up there, I thought Stanley would never believe me unless I could prove it, so I scratched a cross with my fingernail on the white-washed ceiling. My nail left its mark there for anyone to see.

I suppose it took me six weeks of concentrated daily practice to achieve some degree of mastery so that I was able to separate, on my feet, and look down at my body lying prone on the bed. That is it, I thought, now I *know* that there are two of me. I did not need to experiment after that.

Chan's patient tuition, which I had been receiving for some seven years now, came to me in many different ways, always loving, always just what I needed at the time. In the early days when Chan's guidance had come to me through Stanley, it had sometimes been my own subconscious thoughts or inhibitions, even my secret complaints about Stanley, which hid behind the facade of a guide. I did not deceive deliberately. It was total ignorance on my part. Step by step I learned about the possible pitfalls of control. I came to recognise when I could depend implicitly on what was being given to me by Chan and when there was a danger that my own mind would interfere.

It was only gradually that I became aware of how different my work under the sole direction and guidance of Chan was from other mediums and this was borne in on me by the unkind criticisms that sometimes came my way when I started to appear more regularly in public. Chan's complete control of my training was quite different from the usual development circles in which mediums conducted their own development and were the ones who assessed it. I did not at first understand the attitude that I so often encountered, not exactly of animosity but certainly of suspicion.

'Yes, but how do you *know***?'** they would demand, clearly doubting the reality of my guide. Those critics would tell me that guides usually changed the voice, made gestures, altered the stance in some way. This disturbed as well as distressed me, rasing doubts in my own mind which I put to Chan.

'You don't change my voice,' I told him. 'People think I am

only pretending to be in trance.'

It was almost as if I sensed him shrugging his shoulders before he replied. 'I don't care who they think is speaking as long as they listen to what I have to say. It really doesn't matter.'

'It matters to me,' I insisted. 'I need to be sure that I am not deceiving myself or other people.' To this Chan made no reply.

I was getting regular engagements now and the services followed a very regular pattern. The mid-week ones were mainly devoted to clairvoyance and you were expected to keep your address very short. This would be on some philosophical subject and ten minutes was regarded as the maximum, as people really came for the clairvoyance. This I knew very well. Quite soon after raising my doubts with Chan I took the mid-week service at the church in Stratford. At this time I was still working entirely in trance, which itself was very unusual, but I knew no other way. My trance state, however, was far lighter than it became subsequently and I could hear what Chan was saying through me.

That evening started like any other but before it was over I wanted to sink through the floor. Chan came through very quickly and started on the address. So far from proceeding into clairvoyance however, he just continued talking. He talked and he talked. I could hear what was going on, I was aware that the audience, embarrassed at first, were becoming angry, I knew I should have stopped after ten minutes but, try as I would, I could not stop. The coughing and the shuffling of feet became more insistent but still Chan went on talking. It must have been fifty minutes before he stopped talking leaving time for only one message before the service ended.

There was a blackout now and people were anxious to get home. Very clearly they expressed their indignation as they left, and I was covered in embarrassment, not knowing what I could say. Then I heard Chan:

'Now will you believe that I am a separate person?'

'Oh, Chan,' I moaned, 'you need not have done it that way.'

'There was no other way to convince you,' he said.

'Well, I shall never be able to go back to that church again.'

'You won't have to.' And that was his final word.

The very next week that church was bombed out of action. By the time it was repaired nobody remembered that evening except myself, but I was still shaken when I stood up to take the service at another church on the following Sunday night. Mentally, I implored Chan not to go over the usual timing, which was thirty minutes at the Sunday service.

'Look at your watch,' he said. 'It's quarter to seven. At quarter past seven you will be sitting down and they will be singing the hymn before the clairvoyance. Now let me get on with what I have to do.'

And so it was. Ever since then we have had an understanding: according to what we are doing together, with my mind I tell him when we are supposed to finish, and promptly at that time I am sitting down again.

CHAPTER 7

Transfiguration. From trance to clairvoyance. A painful lesson from Chan.

At one of our practice groups at home a sitter thought she saw a face beginning to overshadow mine and commented on it in some excitement. Chan seized on this, immediately asking this person if she would be willing to sit regularly on another night with the aim of developing this aspect of my mediumship. He made it clear that such special sittings would not be occasions for visitors but that an intense degree of concentration would be required from those who were present in order to give their help. This lady agreed to sit regularly with Stanley and my mother, when they would concentrate on building up sufficient power. Transfiguration is a form of mediumship in which an ectoplasmic mask is formed over the medium's face to create a different likeness. It can make the medium look older or younger, or alter the features.

We were given to understand that on the spirit plane the formation of groups to produce physical mediumship is quite a complex matter. Although transfiguration is very different from full materialisation, we were told it is formed with what Chan called the Life Force and was to be treated with the greatest respect. Other guides, too, were needed to take part in developing this; an elderly Chinese man, an Indian and a little Japanese girl.

Darkness was needed for this work except for the very restricted illumination we arranged under Chan's direction; a single red light bulb in a socket below my head at an angle to shine on my face and the area immediately around it. My hair was hidden in a cap so that only my face was visible, forming a screen on which the faces began to form over my own. First the three guides were seen, the formation of each face quite distinct and completely different from the others: the elderly Chinese; then the Indian, who, I understood was in charge of directing the power; and the little Japanese girl. There was also my auric protector, a Sister of Mercy with eyes, even seen in the red light, of a quite distinct light blue, utterly different from my own dark brown ones.

Chan, as he has always done, explained the technicalities behind this form of mediumship. He told us that he himself, working at this level, had to operate on a different vibratory note; for this reason the little Japanese girl helped with the evidence, relaying it to Chan.

As I always worked in trance in those early days Chan would explain to Stanley, my mother and the friend who was helping with the concentration what to expect from each transfiguration.

'This,' he would say, 'is an elderly gentleman. He has a moustache...' and they had to provide the feedback on how successful the manifestations were; was the face old enough, or thin enough, and so on. From this we built up a foundation of transfiguration work in which I became quite proficient.

When I was ready to work publicly in this way Chan

would first give some positive evidence to establish the recipient in the audience. Then he would say he had such and such a person, giving a name and some description or sufficient details of the manner of passing, or the relationship, for identification. When this was acknowledged, Chan would say, 'Now he (or she) is going to try to transfigure and, as we mould the face, I want you to tell me if you want it older or younger.... thinner or rounder....with full or thin lips...' and so on. In the dim red light gradually the mask would be built up until it took on the appearance of the communicator. This was accompanied and supported by the excellent evidence that Chan was always able to provide. It was extremely popular and Chan was very successful in creating transfiguration masks which identified each particular communicator.

My transfiguration work brought me in quite a number of engagements, more than my normal church services and I would often combine the two, a transfiguration on the Saturday or the Monday and on Sunday the usual service. This fitted in well with the difficult wartime conditions of travelling.

At this time the outstanding transfiguration medium lived in Manchester. On one of her visits to a Spiritualist church she had been put up in a damp bed. She developed very severe arthritis and could no longer travel. Transfiguration mediums were rare, so I was in demand. Sadly, I never saw Mrs Bullock myself. It was one of my regrets. She was known to be an extremely nice person, apart from the excellent phenomena she produced. I have no idea whether she presented her transfigurations in the same way as Chan did and it would have interested me deeply to know.

I needed a great deal of encouragement in those early days before I became totally dedicated as I did later. This arose partly because, rightly or wrongly, I felt myself subject to something like jealousy. Perhaps that is not the right word but I was certainly made aware that I was different. It was not that I felt uncertainty about my performance; I knew that my mediumship was entirely acceptable, but I felt isolated by the way in which I worked; something like a fish out of water. Feeling very low, and perhaps a bit sorry for myself, I mentioned to Chan that it would be my birthday on Thursday.

'Yes,' he said, 'I have a little surprise for you. Buy a *Psychic News* next time you go to church.' It so happened that I had a church engagement on the Thursday of my birthday but I knew that Friday was the day when *Psychic News* was available. When I ventured to challenge Chan with this I received no reply. A complete blank. Chan never wasted words.

On arrival at the church on Thursday I was surprised to see copies of Saturday's *Psychic News*. To my even greater surprise it contained a very favourable account of a transfiguration seance I had given. What had particularly impressed this writer was the accuracy of identification each time which extended to the features built up over my face. Normally, with transfiguration mediumship, people with some psychic sensitivity are able to see the faces with greater definition, but on this occasion the changes were quite clearly apparent to all, as I read in this glowing report. I never received a write-up like this again.

My transfiguration work continued alongside my normal trance mediumship for about three years but it did not progress from this high point. It is a form of physical mediumship which makes use of ectoplasm. Some may be drawn from the audience but by far the greater part has to come from the medium. It causes a great strain on the body and on one occasion I had a haemorrhage after working in this way, perhaps because the lights were too strong. Chan explained to me that I did not have the physical stamina to take it further and so after a while it ceased.

Whenever I needed reassurance, as I often did in the early years, Chan would always make sure that I received it without ever letting up on his gentle, but absolutely firm, direction of my development. All the time he was building in those disciplines which have never ceased to be the foundation of our work together. Sometimes this involved the obvious which I could not see; as once when, overwhelmed with zeal to become a really good medium, I asked him what I could do to improve. Very drily, he pointed out that I could start by making a point of arriving at my engagements punctually. Only then did I realise that sometimes, either through domestic pressures or, more rarely, because of some concern of my own, I did arrive in a state of worry lest I should be late. Since then I always made a point of arriving at engagements in good time and Chan was able to depend on this punctuality. Often I received such down-to-earth advice, all given with the unmistakable loving intention of improving our partnership. Never did I feel Chan's comments, pointed as they might be, to be given critically or in any spirit of condemnation.

Chan's tuition came to me in many different ways, always just what I needed at the time. In the early days of development when his guidance came through Stanley it had sometimes been my own subconscious thoughts or inhibitions which hid behind the facade of a guide. I did not deceive deliberately. It was total ignorance on my part. Now I was learning that the medium's thoughts can and sometimes do interfere with those of the guide. Physical thoughts, Chan told me, can be extremely powerful and if a medium holds them strongly they are extremely difficult for spiritual influence to overcome.

As usual, an example soon occurred to bring home this lesson. My mother smoked shags; she rolled her own with the cheapest possible tobacco. She suffered from bronchial asthma and, of course, I knew that smoking was bad for her, but she had so little comfort or pleasure in her life. A young trance medium with whom I was quite friendly asked my mother to sit with her. The guide, some Red Indian, came through emphatically that my mother should not smoke. That was reasonable. However, this girl asked me, a non-smoker, to accompany her for support and whenever I heard her give a sitting her supposed guide always said the sitter should give up smoking. My doubts were confirmed when a sitter who had just been told very forcefully he should not smoke replied that he had never smoked in his life and had no intention of starting.

'That,' explained Chan, 'is prejudice so firmly held in a human mind that spiritual influence cannot erase it.'

I understand that we retain in our subconscious mind every thought and event that we have experienced and that under hypnosis these things can be released. It was explained to me that a somewhat similar release can take place in mediumship. This may, and often does, interfere with communication. On the other hand, what is in the mind of the medium may be completely appropriate to the needs of a particular congregation and it may therefore be this which is released on some occasions. As my understanding grew it did not trouble me to be told that Chan was not there the whole time, although this would really have thrown me before Chan dealt so patiently with my uncertainties. It is this area of mediumship which gives rise to so much mistrust and suspicion of fraud.

I know that Chan sometimes quotes poetry or biblical texts that are in my mind because I loved them and memorised them, alive to their beauty. Chan has always encouraged me to keep extending my vocabulary as he can draw on the words that are in my consciousness. I have always loved language since the inspired teaching of Shakespeare at my school and through the influence of the librarian who guided my reading in those early formative years. My isolated childhood, independent of authority, yet with a firm moral background, was exactly what my spirit friends valued. There have been wonderful mediums who were steeped in orthodoxy but I feel that must to some extent limit the freedom and universality of spiritual truth. It must impede the understanding of a Muslim or a Jew if the medium's expression is in, for instance, orthodox Christian terms; although White Eagle (for one example) does convey that wonderful spiritual quality of love that transcends all limitations. Truth of itself remains unchanged however we may dress it in different robes and disguises.

As part of my training Chan still encouraged me to witness other demonstrations, not to criticise but to observe, and particularly to note any weak spots which prevented their guides from overcoming various forms of interference by the mediums. It seemed to me that a good deal of what I witnessed was certainly not trance in the sense in which I had experienced total control by Chan. Furthermore, some mediums tended to hide behind the authority of their guide in order to cover up mistakes. Chan explained to me that a great deal of what I witnessed was certainly not trance but overshadowing, and he taught me to recognise the change which takes place when the guide takes full possession of the medium by coming into her auric field. When this happens, he explained, the personality of the medium is displaced, rather like sand dropping to the bottom in a glass of water. The guide could now occupy the auric field of the medium and convey the thoughts *he* wanted to relay, while using her physical brain.

This understanding did not come all at once nor was I always able to get my own mind out of the way. It was only step by step, after learning about the possible pitfalls of control, that I came to recognise when I could depend implicitly on what was being given to me by Chan and when there was a danger that I had interfered. Gradually I came to realise that, even on those occasions, I genuinely believed at the time that the thoughts and words were Chan's alone. This understanding has enabled me to recognise that mediums are very rarely consciously fraudulent, though unfortunately they are all too often open to self-deception.

When you have learnt to know the difference, as Chan was able in time to teach me, you always know. I have been on the platform with very well-known and respected mediums and on certain occasions have been aware they were speaking from themselves, not relaying from their guides. What they said was effective and interesting, but it was not the guide, and I *knew*. I remember very well on one such occasion I had been listening more or less mechanically, knowing it was the medium speaking when, just a few minutes before the end, this wonderful quality of love came through her. It was like a cloud, this manifestation of spiritual love, it surrounds and envelops you, and at that moment I knew the difference. Here was the guide, the real guide, and how beautiful he was; so uplifting, one was elevated by his very presence.

That taught me a great deal. Chan had patiently tried to explain to me that these degrees of manifestation are not important of themselves. Our spirit friends have to use us to the level of our capacity to respond to what they are trying to achieve. I do not doubt that my own trance work differs in the levels of Chan's control.

Somehow Chan conveyed to me that you cannot get "better", you can only examine what you are doing to see if it is the best that you can do at that time. If it is, you can expand. If what you are doing is your best, that is the stepping stone to further expansion. There were times when I was very troubled by unkind criticism, because my work was so different from that of other mediums I met. Nobody worked publicly in trance in the way I was doing and sometimes there were sceptical comments – 'I don't believe a guide is there at all' – and so on, which upset me a good deal. Deeply hurt, when I got home I would turn to Chan and repeat these remarks to him.

'Do *you* think it is true?' he would say mildly, 'Look at what you were doing. Did you do everything I asked you to? Did you try to remember what I had said?' If I could honestly answer 'yes' to this gentle probing, Chan would reply, 'Why do you worry about what people think? If it is not true, it does not matter. If it is true, it is helpful to find out because then you can do something about putting it right. There is no need to be hurt, it is God's way of giving you a chance to do better.'

I had been working like this for about three years when I was taking an afternoon service at Woolwich, not transfiguration, just a normal service. It was customary for me to give the address after which, while the hymn was being sung, I would sit down and attune once more before standing up again, when off he would go with the clairvoyance, myself oblivious in trance. On this never-to-be-forgotten afternoon he stunned me when he calmly said, 'You don't need me any more. You can do this for yourself.' I was petrified.

'I can't,' I declared. 'I don't know what to do or where to start.'

'You just get up and give exactly what you get,' was his answer.

I had been to this church several times before and they thought they knew what to expect from me. Now the ground was cut from under my feet. What *was* I going to do? There was nothing else for it, when I stood up, but to say, to their utter astonishment, 'Friends, I don't know what is going to happen. My guide has left me.'

In the bewildered silence that followed I heard Chan say with great confidence, 'Just give what you see and what you hear.'

Looking over the congregation my eye alighted on a particular person and I saw standing beside her the spirit form of a lady. Almost afraid to voice the words, I was starting to describe her when, immediately, with some other part of my brain, I knew that she was the mother of the lady in the congregation. From there I did not look back. The afternoon was a success. When it was over I was so elated that I could not wait until I got home to tell my mother what had happened. The normal charge to telephone from a call box was two pence and I remember being very indignant at having to pay double – four old pennies – because I was telephoning from the other side of the river. When I told my mother how I had been thrown into discovering that I could work in this way she burst into tears!

It was just like Chan to spring this change on me as he did. He never prepared me in any obvious way for the change in my development but he never, ever, let me down. When he said I was ready for some new phase I always was.

One thing that interested me greatly was the coordination which lay behind successful communication. I had often heard mediums saying they would read up on any subject their helpers might want to talk about and I asked Chan if he wanted me to do the same. Most emphatically not, he replied, and went on to explain something of what took place on his level.

The spiritual guardians and helpers of those attending would know, even before the individuals did, that an opportunity for communication was to take place and they would collect up the various people's thoughts. From this pool of information the guide – Chan, in my case – could give messages appropriate to the needs of each recipient of a communication; in fact answering their thoughts. To illustrate this, he cited his own talks when, regardless of the announced topic, those in the audience who were dwelling on some need of their own would receive an answer.

The other factors involved in any service – the thoughts in the mind of the chairperson, the hymns selected, the chosen reading – all these would be orchestrated into an overall theme in which the individual questions of those present would also be relevant.

While I was working in trance I had no say in the matter but when Chan, by his shock tactics at Woolwich, had shown me that I could work as myself, on my own behalf, he explained that trance was not of itself a better way of conveying communication or philosophy, and I found it easier to link with my spiritual friends on an inspirational level without going into trance. Chan advised me not to prepare in any way for my addresses, which were usually required to last not more than twenty minutes. It was far better, he told me, to keep a completely open mind until I was on the platform because I did not know what had been prepared in the unseen realms.

This worried me very much at first. All the people I met in these circles kept saying how necessary it was to know one's subject and it took a great deal of courage for me to take my place on the platform with my mind as blank as I could make it. But again Chan was right, he never let me down. After the reading was finished, he told me, while the congregation were singing the hymn, I should read the passage again to myself.

'When you get to your feet,' he said, 'I will highlight a sentence and the thoughts will flow.'

And so in this way the partnership that I have learned to know and to trust gradually evolved. Later Chan told me that I could incorporate my own experience as this became relevant to the spiritual truth we were seeking to convey. This tailoring to individual needs within a discourse on some general theme is something many people have commented upon and I think that Chan excelled in this. Certainly it always seemed to be remarked upon more in relation to his lectures than to those of other guides.

Some of the lessons Chan had to teach me, however, were still sharp and painful. By now I was enjoying a fair amount of popularity, my clairvoyance was considered exceptional and no doubt I was getting a little cocky. Demonstrating at a very large Spiritualist gathering in Brighton one Sunday evening, I came to a lady who replied 'No' to me three times. This got my goat and I was stung into retorting, 'I don't think I am the right medium for you.' Then I added, 'Next time I am here I shouldn't come, if I were you,' and I continued with the demonstration.

At the end, when the president was making some announcements and I was sitting waiting to give the benediction, I heard Chan say into my ear, 'You were extremely rude and unnecessarily unkind to that lady and you will apologise.'

'Here?' I asked, appalled. 'On the platform?'

'Certainly. You were rude to her in front of all these people and you will apologise in front of them.'

Now it never occurred to me to go against anything Chan told me. The moment came for me to stand up and give the benediction.

'My guide has just told me I was extremely rude to that lady.' I began, when someone shouted, 'Yes, you were!'

'I am extremely sorry, I did not mean to be,' I went on, when this man shouted again, 'I have never heard such rudeness!'

At that, a voice from the other side of the hall broke in with,

'And I have never witnessed such courage. Thank you, Mrs Northage. Shall we have the benediction?'

Afterwards Chan pointed out to me that in the main people come to such services because they are sad or in trouble. They need our help and we must not, under any circumstances, add to their hurt. Very occasionally, when my patience is sorely tried, I may feel a spark of that old – I call it cockiness – but since that day I have made a point of controlling it.

CHAPTER 8

Wartime brings a wider field of work and significant new contacts. First experiences of physical demonstrations. A brush with the Salvation Army. In Devon where her sons had been evacuated to a farm.

After one of my transfiguration meetings I was approached by a Squadron Leader and his wife who expressed a keen interest in this form of mediumship. He was stationed at an American base in Suffolk, not far from a newly formed Spiritualist group in Woodbridge who, they were quite sure, would be delighted to invite me for a demonstration. A weekend was arranged and I was asked to take the Sunday service as well. They would take me in their car and bring me back on the Monday because wartime conditions made such journeys extremely difficult, particularly in East Anglia, centre of so much aircraft activity.

I shall never forget the journey there. I had always been a very poor traveller. When my brother and I were small, my poor mother often had to throw our things away after taking us on a journey, even a long tram ride, because we were so sick. I could not travel any distance without experiencing nausea, followed by sickness. I had never before committed myself to a long car journey and quite soon the nausea started. Horrified that I was going to disgrace myself, I appealed to Chan.

'Shut your eyes,' he said, 'put your head down and just relax.' Desperate, I did this, and it was as if the sickness which I had felt rising to overwhelm me slowed then subsided, and I fell asleep. When I woke up all my nausea had gone and we were well on the way to Woodbridge. The interesting thing is that I never suffered from travelling sickness again, no matter whether on a coach or bus, or for how long. As the war went on I made a great many long and very difficult journeys but never again was I attacked by nausea.

Arrived in Woodbridge, I was greeted warmly by Mr and Mrs Scarfe. He was the President of the newly formed group and had made the church from a converted barn in the garden of their house. I did my demonstration and took the Sunday service, terribly nervous on that first occasion and very, very green. My performance must have been acceptable, however, because Mr Scarfe gave me another engagement and wrote to other people recommending me. They gave me a great deal of encouragement and made me very welcome but the real significance of the visit was the rapport I established with them, starting a friendship which lasted and deepened over the years. By a strange coincidence, the birthdays of their two daughters fell on practically the same days as those of my two sons and the gap between each pair was the same two years.

From our first meeting I received a very great deal of kindness from them both. Physical phenomena were the absorbing interest of Alfred Scarfe and in his desire to learn more he made a point of witnessing as many different physical mediums as he could, inviting them to Woodbridge and often entertaining them in his own home. When Chan told us that I would see every kind of physical manifestation, that kind of seance was far beyond our means and Stanley and I hardly took it seriously. For a long time we could not afford to attend demonstrations for which even a very modest payment was required. However, in the course of time I did, indeed, witness every kind of physical mediumship and not on any occasion did it cost me a penny. Alfred Scarfe was one through whose generosity I received invitations to witness all kinds of demonstrations which otherwise would have been totally beyond my reach.

It seems sometimes to be thought that mediums must be of a refined and spiritual character, at least in some degree, but certainly there are exceptions, as I have discovered to my surprise.

One weekend when I was a guest of Mr and Mrs Scarfe, a medium called Colin had been invited to take the service. On Sunday morning Alfred set out on foot for the station to meet this man and bring him home; no cars at that time, or certainly no petrol for private cars. Meanwhile I, with his wife and two daughters, was preparing lunch. Time went by until, at last, rather late, Alfred returned looking distinctly sheepish and accompanied by a most disreputable man. Alfred was clearly uncomfortable when his wife asked him why they were so late but when he got a moment with her in private he explained: 'Just look at him. I couldn't bring him through the town, I had to take him the long way round.' I don't remember what his service was like but I could never forget his macabre appearance.

The same paradox struck me at a truly remarkable demonstration of levitation. The medium had a most unprepossessing appearance; his suit was stained, his hair unkempt and his face unshaven. He must have weighed fifteen stone. Our chairs had been arranged in a circle and the medium's chair, an obviously very strong one of solid wood, semi-circular, with arms which curved round his body, had been painted with luminous paint. Then two men came forward from the audience to strap him in. They did this very thoroughly, tying his arms with rope to the arms of the chair and his feet to the legs. When all this was completed to their satisfaction and we could see that the medium was securely bound to the chair, all the lights were extinguished.

We sat for a while in the dark. Some music was played and we could just distinguish the bulk of his form in the centre and the dim shadows of those making up the large circle around him, all completely out of his reach. Presently we saw the chair, with this enormous man in it, begin to ascend. As it gradually rose higher we could see the luminous paint on the soles of his shoes. It was a totally extraordinary experience to watch this heavy man, together with the solid wooden chair, with no tangible means of propulsion, rise up until his head was touching the ceiling. No communication took place. It was a purely physical demonstration reversing the law of gravity, an exhibition of levitation powered by an unknown source of energy.

Sitting there I could hear again in my mind that medium saying from the platform, 'Your guide is saying that you will witness every form of mediumship so that when you stand up on any platform you can say "I have seen this, I know it is true, it is not something I have only read about." '

At another meeting I met this medium's wife. She had the same dishevelled appearance as he did except for her hair, naturally golden and piled on top of her head in a coronet. Despite her otherwise unkempt appearance she spoke in a cultured voice, in fact she had a university degree. Telling me that her hair was the one thing of which she was really proud, she asked if I would like to see it. When she took the combs out and let it down, it fell to her thighs in a golden cascade. I have never seen anything like that hair, so beautiful, and the rest of her such a contrast; her clothes were stained, her nails neglected and dirty, her whole appearance a travesty of that glorious head of hair.

When I had occasion to visit their home, a large mansion flat, the same impression of dirt and disorder was overwhelming. The rooms were large with good big windows but it was the squalor which hit one in the eye, an incredible conglomeration of litter: wastepaper baskets spilling over with unemptied rubbish, trays of unwashed teacups, plates and glasses, all kinds of household rubbish waiting to be cleared away. Piled onto a grand piano, itself covered in dust, were stacks of books, jars with pens in them, packets of paper. I could not imagine how such disorder and squalor could go hand in hand with this medium's truly amazing physical mediumship and his wife's clairvoyance.

One morning a letter arrived from the Salvation Army saying they had a very serious matter to discuss with me. Sally was now trotting about and Dolly had been visiting us for about eighteen months. The appointment was before her next visit so I could not ask her if she knew what it was about. I thought perhaps she was ill when I set out for the Salvation Army Headquarters in Hackney, not very far from where we were living. I was directed towards an office and shown into a very pleasant room with a lady sitting behind a desk. She was in uniform, her bonnet and jacket on a stand. I was struck by how beautiful she was, with glorious chestnut hair piled up in an Edwardian style, a perfect complexion and lovely eyes.

Her first words took me by surprise. 'You realise, of course, why I have asked you to come?'

'No,' I replied, 'I have no idea.'

'But surely Lunden has been to see you?' (That was Dolly's surname, they never used her Christian name.)

'Yes, she has been coming every week.'

'And you really don't know that she is *pregnant* again?'

This astonished me. I had truly noticed nothing at all and I felt something of a shock. Before I had fully absorbed this news I heard her voice continue (a beautiful cultured voice), 'You will realise of course that we are turning her out. You will tell her to take her baby and they are both going to the workhouse.'

This really shocked me. I looked at her. She was quite serious.

'I beg your pardon,' I said.

'You will do exactly as I say. You will tell Lunden that she must take her baby now and they will both go to the workhouse.'

I have never been one to take orders. When this lady said 'You *will* do this' my hackles rose. Kicking away the chair I was sitting on, I stood up so that I was looking down on her. 'How dare you tell me what I am to do with my own domestic arrangements?' I demanded.

'We are turning her out,' she repeated. 'We will have

nothing more to do with her. You may not realise this is the third time this has happened.'

I did know that this was the third time because I had visited Dolly's people. When Philip was convalescing from a severe illness my mother-in-law took him to Eastbourne and I had an engagement in Woodbridge, not far from Lowestoft. Someone had made me a present of five pounds so I took Derek with me for him to have a little holiday too, and after Woodbridge we went to Lowestoft. There I met Dolly's mother with this little girl, about six years older than Sally, skipping around, and I knew that she was the reason why Dolly had been sent to London in the first place. The most inexplicable thing to me; poor Dolly had a face like the back of a bus and no attraction at all that I could ever see.

'I don't know much about your religion, Major,' I retorted, 'but I do know a little about Christian teaching. Jesus said we were to forgive not seven times but seventy times seven and that is a long way to go after three. I will not ask her to take the baby away. I will not let her be sent to the workhouse and if you turn her out *I* will give her a home.'

She argued with me, insisting that I was encouraging Dolly in sin. I thought, how can so beautiful a person – she really was beautiful – be so bigoted and so hard.

Dolly was duly turned out and I took her in. She told me nothing at all about the man or the circumstances, then or at any time; she was the most silent, uncommunicative creature. My mother was as surprised as I. When Dolly came to visit she would arrive about three o'clock and leave at six. My mother would give her tea and they would chat but we never, ever learned anything about her life outside those three hours a week. Although Dolly was six months pregnant at the time the Mothers' Hospital turned her out, it did not show. Stanley was away in the army and I slept alone in our bedroom. We accommodated Dolly with a camp bed at the foot of mine.

Soon after this the Welfare visitor with whom I was on friendly terms paid us a visit and I explained why Dolly was now living with us. Arrangements had been made for her to have the baby at Forest Gate, not too far from Leytonstone where we were living. Very fortunately, as it turned out, the Welfare visitor, after saying she thought it extremely generous of me to take Dolly in, urged me very strongly to make it clear that this was a temporary arrangement which would cease when Dolly went into hospital for the birth. 'Make it quite clear when she goes in that there is nowhere for her to go after the birth. They will have to provide for them then, but otherwise you will be landed.'

When I explained all this to Dolly she accepted it quite placidly, uncommunicative as ever. She was like a piece of wood sometimes, one never felt really in contact with her. The weeks went by, still in this totally uncommunicative way until one night in September. We had been sitting together and went to bed as usual at about half past ten, Dolly saying nothing. It was around midnight when she woke me to announce,

'I think I have to go to the hospital.'

'What, *now*?' I queried.

'Yes,' she replied, 'I have been having pains all the evening and they are getting much worse. I have to go.'

'Oh, Dolly,' I said, exasperated in spite of myself, '*why* didn't you say earlier. There are no buses now, no transport.

We'll have to walk.'

It was about two and a half miles to the hospital from our house and of course I could not let her go alone. There was nothing for it but to get up and get dressed and together we set out. In one of the quiet turnings on our way I noticed a little black kitten following us, keeping just a few yards behind us as we walked. It followed us all the way to the hospital. At the gates I tried again to send it back, saying aloud, 'You can't come in here, you'll get lost.' As if it understood, it settled down to wait.

It had taken us about an hour to walk to the hospital. By the time all the formalities had been completed and I had seen Dolly settled in, it was three o'clock in the morning when I left to start the long walk home. At the gate the little black kitten was waiting just where I had left it and it followed me all the way home. I had not the heart to turn it away so I let it come into the house before falling into bed, exhausted. When my mother came in with a cup of tea in the morning, 'There must be a cat in the house,' she said. 'I don't know how it got in but I can hear it.' We found it in the cellar. As a family we were devoted to cats and that happened to be a time when we did not have one so we adopted it and it lived with us for many years.

At the time of the first bomb scare we had not considered evacuation for the boys but as the bombing intensified, and we were in line with the docks, we felt we ought to let them go; so, against their wishes, Philip and Derek were evacuated to a farm on Exmoor. Sally, nearly two, was too young and my mother preferred to stay in London. I was busy now with my mediumship, travelling the country as far as wartime conditions allowed. As soon as I could I determined to go and see the boys to make sure they were being properly looked after.

The farmer's wife agreed to put me up and they arranged to meet my train at South Moulton, the nearest station, at five o'clock; it was due to arrive at that convenient time. However, wartime travelling knew no rules and after an utterly nightmarish journey the train arrived at nearly one o'clock in the morning. Of course no-one was there to meet it. I and a few other stranded passengers were rescued by the kindness and hospitality of the George Hotel who not only let us sit in the lounge for what remained of the night but provided blankets for us. In the morning they gave us breakfast for which they made no charge. Those who lived through the war remember, as well as the destruction and the horrors, the many spontaneous acts of kindness, the fellow feeling which so often showed itself during those dark years.

The farm at Simmons Bath was thirteen miles away with no telephone. At last the hotel porter managed to find a taxi which had the petrol and was willing to take me there. The school was in the village, two miles away from the farm, and when I arrived the boys were still there; they stayed all day because it was too far for them to come back for lunch. The farmer's wife – she originally came from Essex – greeted me in a quite normally civil and friendly way but her husband, when he appeared, was most uncouth. He did not utter a word to me.

When Derek and Philip came back in the late afternoon all the family went to their places at a huge, long table for the evening meal; the farmer and his wife, a sister-in-law who was saying there with her little boy, myself and my two boys. Last came the two farm hands. After removing their wellington boots they sat a little apart at the end of the table. From the moment I saw Derek and Philip come in I was troubled, they seemed so subdued. Neither spoke a word, they hardly even said hello to me, and Derek was a naturally talkative boy. The farmer's wife tried very hard to make some conversation, asking me a bit about myself and saying how trying the journey must have been. No-one else spoke. The boys sat completely silent. By now it was getting dusk. The room was lighted only by an acetylene lamp in the centre of the table, controlled, like our gas lighting in those days, with a chain.

As soon as we had finished eating, the farmer's wife gathered together the dishes, brought in a basin of water and proceeded to wash them up at the table. Wishing to make myself agreeable, I took up a cloth and dried them, handing them to her to put away. When we had finished I sat down again and so did she. No-one had been talking while this took place, the heavy silence was becoming more and more oppressive. Suddenly the farmer got up. He still did not say a word but everyone, including Philip and Derek – everyone except me – got up. The two farm workers had shuffled out the moment the meal was ended, before the washing-up. The farmer pulled the chain and the lamp went out. Not a word was spoken, not even to say good-night. There was nothing for me to do but follow suit.

Mine was a weekend visit so the boys were not at school and I became more and more concerned because they were so silent. When I took them for a walk in the fields and remarked on this they just shrugged and muttered 'nothing to say'. A man who passed the farm on his way to the village picked them up each morning for school so they had to leave very early. By the time they came home it was late afternoon and they were met with this total lack of communication.

On this short visit I did not have time to do much but I determined to see if there was any possibility of improving their situation. On the Monday when I met them from school I learnt that the estate was privately owned, and opposite the village hall where the children went to school was a hunting lodge to which a private girls' school from Bognor had been evacuated for the duration of the war. If I could get a job there, I thought, I could see the boys not only when they came out from school but I could also spend their two free hours at lunchtime each day with them. From what I had seen I felt it would take me all of this to bring them back to their normal cheerful selves.

I have never hesitated to pursue an aim so, my mind made up, I lost no time in asking to speak to the Principal of the evacuated school. After explaining the situation and making it clear that I wanted something temporarily, I asked if there was any chance of a job.

'I'm sorry,' she said, 'but the only thing I can offer you is kitchen work. Paula would be most grateful for help but it is very, very menial.'

'What, exactly, would I be expected to do?'

'All you would have to concern yourself with is lighting the fires in the morning, washing the pots and pans, and perhaps helping Cook to peel the vegetables.'

When I replied that washing dishes and doing vegetables

was not very different from what I did for my family, she smiled a little wryly.

'I think, my dear, you will find it different, but I admire your courage.' Then she added: 'And I will arrange that when your children are free from school, you shall be free to spend with them such time as they are able to stay in the village.'

She was as good as her word, arranging this with the housekeeper, and so I was able to spend time regularly with Derek and Philip, building up contact again and trying to lighten their spirits. But the work! The pots and pans were indeed different from family life; they were so huge that I could have got inside them. Furthermore they were copper, and not only did they have to be cleaned but polished. And the attack on the vegetables! About eighty or ninety girls were boarding with quite a numerous staff so the mountains of vegetables were huge.

We were housed in what had been the stables, about twelve of us in a dormitory which was in some kind of shed. The beds were quite comfortable and my mother sent me a sweet ration and a few little luxuries that I was able to share with Derek and Philip. I kept these in a carrier bag beside my bed. To my utter horror I woke up one night to see an enormous rat coming out of the bag, poised to jump on my bed. That was the end of living in on the job for me, but I did not go straight home. I was able to sleep at the farm and get a lift in each day, not with the boys but through a builder at the end of the lane. He used to go into the village at around that time and he said if I liked to be there he would give me a lift. It was a farm vehicle, not designed to carry passengers, and I had to sit on his lap. He did get a little fresh sometimes, but nothing out of hand, and I was extremely grateful to be able to continue with the job for a while and build up the contact with my sons.

But the job! That was quite an experience in itself, not only the physical stamina needed but the strict hierarchy observed in the kitchen. Cook, of course, was supreme there and when the Principal of the school came in to give her orders for the day all the rest of us kitchen staff had to leave the room. When we saw the Principal leave, that was the cue for us to file back and get on with our various jobs.

I stayed for about a month before going home to London and my mother. She was still keeping house for me and it was thanks to her that I was free not only to make this visit to the boys but to travel to the mediumship engagements I was offered.

Dolly, meanwhile, had returned to Lowestoft. Her third baby was another girl. I was very grateful to the Welfare visitor who warned me not to have them back after the birth because it was six months before the baby was adopted. They called her Ivy and I understand she went to a wealthy family in Romford, which pleased Dolly very much.

There was an interesting sequel to my visit to the farm and it was not many months later that Derek and Philip came home for good.

CHAPTER 9

More materialisation seances. Recollections of Helen Duncan. Other remarkable physical mediumship.

An outstanding physical medium whose work I saw through the hospitality of Alfred Scarfe was Ronald Strong. He was a young man and his appearance, again, was very off-putting. His suit was not dirty, as Colin's had been, but it was unpressed and his shirt was crumpled, his hair needed trimming and altogether he looked very neglected and as if he needed a shave. I used to wonder why physical mediums all seemed to be so unkempt and whether it was something to do with the exhaustion inseparable from producing physical phenomena that made them so careless of their appearance.

Although Ronald was only in his early twenties at this time he was already quite well known and his seances had been reported favourably in *Psychic News*. He was billed as a direct voice medium; that is, the voice coming through him is audible to everyone to a greater or lesser degree according to the quality, whereas in clairaudience and clairvoyance the voice is heard by the medium inside his head and he then has to speak the words. In direct voice mediumship the sound is frequently enhanced by the use of a metal trumpet, cone-shaped, wide at one end and narrow at the other, and the voices are spoken through the narrow end. Such trumpets have luminous paint at each end so that in the dark you can see them darting about to find the intended recipient for each communication. Ronald Strong did not have his own trumpet but most Spiritualist churches had this equipment.

Alfred had offered me the booking for the service that week-end, inviting me at the same time to sit in at Ronald's demonstration before I went home. This was most considerate and generous of him, because not only did I not have to pay the entrance fee, I would be paid, however modestly, for taking the service beforehand, and, more importantly, my fare was paid. Ronald arrived with his retinue of two very overdressed ladies and one man in time for lunch with the Scarfes to which I also was invited. I was to take the service in the afternoon and Ronald was to give his seance in the evening. He, of course, had no interest in attending a service with an unknown medium like myself giving the clairvoyance, so he and his three supporters spent the afternoon exploring Woodbridge which was indeed a very pretty place.

Only one item from my afternoon was remarkable and that only because of what happened afterwards. During my demonstration of clairvoyance I had given news of a much-loved pet, a dog called Prince. I was able to say that the communicator wanted the owner to know that Prince was being looked after and was waiting – that sort of message. I have found that people are often more delighted with the return of their pets than they are with their relatives, but that is another story. As I have said, Ronald was not present. Nor was this message – or of course any message I had received –

mentioned afterwards.

We were joined at tea by a Mrs Truscott who had come from Ipswich to be present at the seance in the evening. She was a great benefactor to the Woodbridge Spiritualist Church, which she greatly preferred to the one in Ipswich, and so she was always invited to take part in any special event. At the tea the talk was naturally about physical phenomena and Mrs Truscott mentioned that she had twice been to Edinburgh to sit in a group with Helen Duncan but that upon neither of these occasions had she herself received anything.

For the evening seance the chairs had been arranged in a very large circle and we sat in darkness, some twenty-five of us. You could just make out the deeper black of the sitters' bodies. It would have been easy to see if anyone moved but in this pervading darkness the only points of light were the luminous trumpets, one at either side of the very large circle of chairs but not close enough for anyone to reach out and touch them. We sang together for some time. As I understand it, singing is part of the process of changing the vibrations. After a while we heard a voice greeting us, a beautiful bass voice, entirely different from Ronald's which was unmistakably effeminate. Indeed, I had found Ronald most offensively effeminate when we met. The voice announced that he was Red Feather and that he was going to bring as many of our loved ones as he could by this means and went on to explain how he needed our support and our responses. Then he said, 'Where is the lady officiating this afternoon?'

In a timorous voice I said, 'Here I am, Red Feather,' and I saw the trumpet coming gently toward me. Now, I cannot bear to be touched, so with my mind I tried to ward it off. This was almost an automatic reaction when I saw it coming at me, but immediately it stopped and I heard the same beautiful deep voice say, 'There is someone here who wants to say a very real thank you to you for restoring him to those he loved, and who loved him. Come along, Prince.' And the dog barked, the resonant bark of a large dog. We heard him bark twice.

This, in that hushed seance room, was quite extraordinary. I was only sad because Prince's owner was not there. Ronald Strong's seances were certainly not cheap and a great many people would not have been able to afford them.

Other communication followed and then a different voice was heard, still a man's voice but not with the positive resonance of Red Feather. This one was still cultured but rather hesitant and then it faded out. In the pause that followed someone in the circle said, 'I thought he said he was Albert.'

'Isn't that Mrs Duncan's guide?' remarked someone else. After another, longer pause, 'Oh, look!' said someone, 'I think he is trying to build up.' I was sitting next to Alfred and I asked if he could see anything.

'I can see something,' he said. 'It looks like a long, thin streak.' I could see nothing myself and almost at once it was gone.

Then we heard this same voice ask, 'Where is the lady who was so disappointed on her visits to Edinburgh?' After Mrs Truscott had confirmed her presence, the voice, almost as if with difficulty, continued, 'I am sorry you were disappointed when you visited my medium in Edinburgh but next time you come I will see that you are not disappointed again.'

Mrs Helen Duncan's guide, Albert, was known to be forthright and extremely caustic though I had not until that moment had direct experience of him. His usual method of communication was by materialisation. The voice was certainly not Red Feather's and I immediately began to wonder if this was Ronald interfering, because I knew that he had heard that at the tea table. However, that my suspicion was unfounded became evident on a later occasion in a very unexpected way.

From my first introduction to the Woodbridge Spiritualist circle Chan had become well known to Alfred and his friends. Practising with them under Chan's direction had been an important phase in my development and he was quite familiar to them all. When a fresh voice now said, 'Good evening,' someone asked who it was. The reply, in those distinctive and courteous tones, 'Have I been with you so long and yet you do not know me? Where is my medium?' was so unexpected, my heart nearly stopped beating.

Again I saw the trumpet coming towards me until it was about a yard away, when, with my mind, I said 'stop' and it stopped. In a seance of this kind you have to keep a conversation going, otherwise the power flags and the trumpet collapses, so you are encouraged to say whatever comes into your head. Largely to avoid one of these gaps I asked if Philip and Derek were all right. 'Oh, yes,' he said, 'they are perfectly all right. You can have them home at any time now, the danger is over.'

Now that had not for a moment been in my mind. It was not at all what I had been contemplating. I let it go because I was concerned with my development as a medium and wanted to hear more about that. 'There are no problems with that,' he told me; then very solemnly: 'I want to assure you that while I promise you no fame or glory, we shall serve humanity together. Of that I give you my solemn word.'

This is the only time Chan ever talked to me directly. He talked about our work together and the plans he had for me and how pleased he was that I was persevering with my development.

Whenever my mind turned to it through the years I could hear again that cultured, gentle voice with its solemn promise that has helped me again and again through the dark patches – some of them very dark indeed – which lay ahead, although I knew nothing of them at the time.

When I arrived home on the Monday, a letter was waiting for me from Derek, the younger one. 'Dear Mummy, Please, please, please (underlined), please come and take us home. The lady here is having a baby and they are going to put us in the work-house.' Derek was an avid reader and I think he must have been reading *Oliver Twist*.

I had in fact known about the coming baby because while I was visiting the farm the farmer's wife asked if I would come and look after her husband and the children while she was having the baby. Of course I had explained my own commitments but I had no idea that they would ask the authorities to take my sons. Things were really hotting up in London then and without Chan's assurance I would not have felt able to take the responsibility of bringing the children back to the bombing. Thanks to him, however, I was able with a clear conscience to fetch my sons and bring them home. We had a few hair-raising experiences with windows blown out on several occasions but no serious damage to the house. Had I not received reassurance from Chan so unexpectedly that evening I would have been sorely troubled.

The wonderful way in which one is supported at exactly the right moment – not before, not after, but just when it is needed – has been borne in on me very much more clearly over the years. I did not have this understanding then but I was profoundly grateful that Chan had let me know what to do.

About two years after the Ronald Strong seance I had attended in Woodbridge he was instrumental in my witnessing another demonstration of the most amazing physical phenomena. He, with his own physical group, had been developing further in the intervening period and my mediumship also had grown and was more in demand. My engagements did not leave me much time but Ronald wrote to say he had the chance of sitting with Mrs Helen Duncan who was coming to London on a visit and asking if I would put him up for the night. He had arranged for me to accompany him to the seance.

There were some seven or eight of us in a room in a private house. I had not previously met Mrs Duncan. My only experience of her guide, Albert, was that brief intervention of his in Woodbridge when it was thought that he was trying to materialise but no more than a wisp of ectoplasm had manifested. Mrs Duncan was a most remarkable materialisation medium but stories had got around that she secreted butter muslin on her person and produced this to fake ectoplasm. On this evening two of the ladies who had come to witness the demonstration took her to another room and stripped her, bringing her back clothed only in a loose garment made of black-out material, when they solemnly testified that the medium had no material of any kind on her person.

The seance took place in red light and, as we were so few, there was just one small semi-circle of chairs not far from the medium.

It was usual for physical mediums to work in a cabinet and one had been rigged up in this room with black curtains hung across a corner, closed except for a gap of about eight inches through which we could see Mrs Duncan. She was a big woman, we could not see all of her, but there was a clear view of her body and we saw ectoplasm streaming out of it in billowing folds. These then appeared to give a little shiver, whereupon we saw the figure of a very tall man in white robes – a somewhat arabic effect. His head, too, was swathed in white. I think that was to conserve ectoplasmic substance. In contrast, his face was extremely clear with well-defined features: sharp nose, thin mouth and high cheekbones, very dark, deeply-set eyes, moustache and Van Dyke beard.

Albert was fully materialised; you felt you could have put out your hand and touched him, though of course that was never allowed. He exuded an air of distinction. When he spoke it was in a cultured voice, utterly different from the very rough Scottish accent of Mrs Duncan. From his great height you got the feeling that he was not exactly bending over us but talking down to us.

Among the sitters was Alfred Scarfe who had invited me to attend Ronald Strong's demonstration after I took the service at Woodbridge church some two years previously. Albert turned to him and declared somewhat caustically, 'I have been called many things in my time but *never* have I been referred to as a long, thin streak.'

Alfred, who had entirely forgotten the incident, was taken aback and completely at a loss until I whispered, 'Woodbridge – Ronald Strong and the direct voice,' when, in considerable embarrassment, he said, 'Oh, yes. I am so sorry.'

'No need to be sorry,' said that autocratic voice. 'That was what you saw and it was perfectly in order for you to speak about what you saw. I just wanted you and the lady with you to know that you are the only person who has referred to me in that way. Unless I *had* been there I could not have told you about it, could I?'

I was afraid that Albert would mortify me by adding 'And *you* did not believe that it was I.' That was quite true, but to my relief he did not say anything to me at all. He continued talking to Alfred. 'You are sitting for direct voice?' After Alfred confirmed this he asked, 'Would you recognise the trumpets that you use in Woodbridge?'

'Certainly I would,' replied Alfred. 'They have my own special mark on them.'

Again there was a whoosh and a clatter (one always heard this peculiar whooshing sound before a physical manifestation) and there were two trumpets, one longer than the other. 'Pick them up,' said Albert. Alfred picked up each trumpet in turn, looked around it and saw the unobtrusive identifying signs with which he had marked his own trumpets and which no-one in the room would have known. This was striking enough but then Albert said they would try to bring them his mother.

Albert then disappeared. It was a very fast thing, this appearing and disappearing. Materialisations do not dissolve or go behind the curtain; it is as if one second they are there and the next they are gone. Then came a rustling of the curtain as if it was being moved gently by breezes – there were always these little shakes and shivers – and there was Albert's mother, a short figure with a rather lined face. 'I have come all the way from Woodford to see you,' she said. Now this was not quite accurate. Alfred lived in Woodbridge, but he obviously recognised her and a great deal of personal and family information further identified her, as I myself could see. At the end of their talk she seemed to lose height, then there was this peculiar shudder and she was gone.

In the course of the seance various people materialised, relatives and friends of the sitters. Some of the manifestations were so extraordinary that I could not have believed them unless I had seen them myself. One lady came with a rabbit on her arm, a perfect miniature rabbit no more than three inches long. As it turned its head, looking round with bright little eyes, Albert addressed one of the sitters. 'This is one of your pets, isn't it?' 'Oh, yes,' she replied, 'We used to call her Minnie.'

Most sensational of all was a miniature baby materialised for a sitter who had only that week lost a baby of a few months.

My father said hello to me but nothing else. I never saw him materialise, I only heard his voice behind the curtain.

After the others had left, our host invited me and Alfred to stay on so that we could meet Helen Duncan when she had recovered. Exhausted as she was, she was nevertheless very friendly and Alfred persuaded her to visit Woodbridge professionally, which she did on several occasions. I attended her demonstrations twice in London but never received anything else myself through her, possibly because the vibratory note between us was not quite right on that level. Personally she was always most friendly to me and I came to know her quite well through our meetings in Woodbridge. She was often in and out of hospital and had to undergo an operation for ulcers. While she was convalescing at the home of Alfred and Ethel Scarfe we had a good many talks together.

She told me that after the operation the surgeon came to her in bed, his manner curious. 'Tell me,' he enquired, 'Do you eat a normal diet?' Nellie was extremely rough in her speech and very outspoken; there were always a few adjectives thrown in.

'What do you mean about my …. diet?' she demanded.

'Well,' he replied, 'when we opened you up we found cigarettes, papers, cigarette ends, toffee papers, we found all sorts of bits of fluff and dirt – it made us wonder.'

When, subsequently I was able to ask Chan about this he explained to me that the ectoplasm going out from her body trailed on the floor before it took form or disintegrated, picking up any loose bits of debris on the way. The ectoplasm, which is life matter, then flashes back (that is the shudder or shiver one always saw) into the solar plexus before being renewed and released again for the next materialisation. Nellie told me of another occasion when someone had suddenly switched the lights on; when she went to dress and took off her black robe the whole of her stomach was black, as if with a very bad blood blister, the blood congealed and dark.

How I admired her work. Apart from her most exceptional gift she was really a very foolish woman and I used to tell her how silly she was to allow her family to depend on her in the way they did. She had no money, poor woman, apart from what she could earn from her mediumship. She was a really wonderful medium judged by the true quality of her work but she did not obey Albert's instructions for protecting and fostering her great gift.

Physical mediumship is always a tremendous strain on the body but Helen Duncan took no care of hers; she pushed herself beyond the limits of her physical vitality. To produce materialisations takes a very great deal of physical energy and, overworked, sometimes exhausted as she was, often she did not have enough. It was explained to me that if there is not sufficient power to produce a full materialisation the spirit guides will make use of what there is in the best way they can. With Helen Duncan, when the power was insufficient through her physical exhaustion, they would use what ectoplasm there was as a clothing, or mask, rather like my own transfiguration work. It would be possible to form to a degree the likenesses of those who were trying to communicate, but it was not a solid form, not true materialisation and she herself would be out of her chair and seen to be so by the sitters who, in their ignorance, attributed this to fraud. What these people did not understand was that our spirit helpers will never fail to produce what they can out of whatever is made available to them.

I was able to observe this for myself on another occasion when the power was low and she was not at her best. It is difficult to describe, but the materialisations were not solid in the way I had witnessed before. I distinctly remember the only partially materialised form of a nun, her arms held out; the draperies hanging down were transparent and limp, they looked like pieces of material with no arms to support them, so utterly different from the quality of her mediumship on that first occasion I was so privileged to witness.

On the day she was physically seized upon in the middle of a seance by police claiming to catch her in mid-fraud, Albert had warned her in the morning. 'Don't go,' he had urged. 'Do not go.' But for Helen the money she received from these demonstrations, and it could be a great deal by her standards, was a great temptation; not for herself, but for her family. She worked herself to death. When I visited her home in Edinburgh everything shone with cleanliness. It was she who kept the home and whenever she returned after an engagement she would be working to get it in order again.

I did not see her after she came out of prison; she did not live very long after that. It was all so sad and unnecessary[1].

---

[1] *Helen Duncan's case has received a good deal of recent publicity but it is difficult to see how, after this lapse of time, evidence could be forthcoming which would clear her name in a court of law. Equally, no-one has been able to explain how she produced the facts of the sinkings which led to her conviction. One book on this subject is* "Medium on Trial: The True Story of Helen Duncan and the Witchcraft Act" *by Manfred Cassirer. Psychic News Publishing, 1996.*

The difference between the guides of various mediums was striking. Helen Duncan's guide, Albert, was imposing and distant in his manner. I believe he had been an Oxford don and his cultured voice, with its distinctive diction, could sound very caustic. Nothing could have been more different from the medium's very rough, broad Scottish accent. His greeting never conveyed warmth or even any quality of impersonal love; in this so different from Ursula Robert's guide, Ramadan, and of course from my own dear Chan, whose special quality is unmistakable: a lovely, cool detachment, completely devoid of emotion which yet never fails to convey his personal caring. Ronald Strong's Red Feather spoke with a rich resonance, giving the impression of a very powerful personality.

Some of his medium's feats were certainly powerful. One I remember vividly took place at Woodbridge. For these physical seances the chairs were arranged in a circle on the floor. On a higher level, at one end, was the platform with the usual rail in front, a curtain and a reading desk and chair. Ronald sat in a chair in the centre of the circle, a length of rope beside him. Red Feather had apparently indicated earlier that he would need this. When the seance started we heard Red Feather say, 'Do we have a naval captain present?'

Woodbridge of course is near to the sea. When a very burly man in civilian clothes answered that he was a sea captain, Red Feather asked if he was proficient in the special seafarers' knots which cannot be undone.

'Oh, yes,' said this man, 'I had to know all that and you never lose it,' whereupon he received his instructions.

'Will you take this length of rope and tie this young man to the chair. I want you to tie him by the ankles and by his arms, his wrists and his elbows. Then I want you to take the rope round his body, beneath his shoulder blades, and tie it at the back of the chair as firmly as you can.' This procedure took some time before the sea captain was satisfied that Ronald was totally secured to the chair. We were sitting in a red light now and Ronald was in a deep trance.

'Put out the light,' said Red Feather.

In the sudden blackness we heard a peculiar whooshing noise, rather like the rushing wind in a tunnel, and then a very slight bump, followed by the voice of Red Feather.

'Put on the light.'

To our utter amazement, there was poor Ronald on the platform. This was at least three feet higher than the level of the floor and Ronald, completely bewildered, was sitting on the chair that had been up there all the time while the chair he had been tied to, still with the rope intact but empty, remained where it had been – on the floor in the centre of the circle.

The dramatic effect of this was overwhelming.

During these years I myself was doing transfiguration work and always the first to show was a very old Chinese guide. His face would overlay mine and he would cause my mouth to open, showing quite clearly his toothless gums, whereas I had all my own teeth. At another of Ronald Strong's seances Red Feather said that he could not conjure up enough power to form an ectoplasmic mask but that he would do his best. In the red light in which we were sitting a kind of replica of my Chinese guide could be seen, as if formed in burnt paper. The long, thin moustache was there, together with the very high cheekbones and domed head. This black burnt paper mask – as it seemed – floated around the circle.

Most of those present had seen my transfiguration work and so were familiar with my guide. This was the nearest approach to anything like personal evidence which I received through Ronald Strong and it was the last time I saw him. He was known to be somewhat degenerate as a person and I heard that he went from bad to worse and died, in poverty, in his thirties.

CHAPTER 10

Ivy's father and some striking evidence. Materialisations and apports. An embarrassing prank.

It was not often at these physical phenomena seances that I myself received a communication but one curiously evidential message was given to me by the direct voice medium, Louisa Bolt. She had been very successful for a well-known family who had lost a son in the war. In the ensuing publicity she had been hounded by the press and retired to live very quietly, giving only a few quite private sittings. Alfred Scarfe took me to one of these at her flat in Ravenscourt Park. Her much older companion had something he called an amplifier – a miniature amplifier. This equipment was pivoted on a sapphire, with a needle, and in the darkness the light from the sapphire flashed, directing its ray towards the recipient of the communication.

As the beam from the sapphire flashed towards me I heard a voice say,

'I have someone called George for you. He says he is your father.'

Now my father's name, as far as I knew, was Henry, and I was about to disclaim the name when the unmistakable voice of my father greeted me. (As I have explained, his voice was exactly like my brother's, a very distinctive voice, and this enabled me to recognise my father, although I had never met him.) When I asked him why he had announced himself as George, he replied that it was because it was his name.

'I am George Henry,' he added.

'But surely,' I demurred, 'Henry is your first name?'

'No,' he retorted. 'Look at the papers at home and you will see.'

Then he said, 'Listen to this,' and he whistled a tune of five notes. He made me whistle it after him to make sure I had it correctly. 'Give my love to your mother,' he said. 'Whistle that tune and ask her why I came back with that. Tell her I am always with her.' And then he was gone.

My mother shared my surprise at the name my father had given until we looked at her marriage certificate and there it was: George Henry Fitzpatrick. Everyone always called him Henry, however, and she had never thought of him as George. I had never known him by that name. When I whistled those five little notes she burst into tears.

My mother as a girl lived with her grandparents in Soho. They were connected with the theatre and I believe they let the upper part of their house. The living room and kitchen were in the basement and that is where the family would be during the daytime. My father, a youth then, was a pageboy in one of the nearby hotels and considered by my grandparents to be quite unsuitable for their daughter who was not allowed to go out with him. Every afternoon during his hours off duty he would saunter past the basement area whistling that tune, the signal for my mother to find some pretext, an errand to run, some excuse, to slip out and spend the time with him until he had to return to his hotel. That tune, which my mother was so understandably thrilled to hear again, was an astonishing piece of evidence.

At this same seance, evidence of a totally different kind, equally remarkable, was received by Alfred. First he was told to hold out his hand, quite flat; then to curl it up like a fist to keep it closed. When some moments later he was asked if he could feel anything, he said it was getting very hot.

'Hold on,' he was told. 'Don't open your hand yet.'

'But it's burning me,' protested Alfred, obviously very uncomfortable. Still he was told to hold on.

When, at last, he was allowed to open it, there inside his hand was a tiny miniature boat, the kind to put on a charm bracelet. As we were all gazing at this in astonishment, we heard the voice say, 'Your mother says that is the answer to your advertisement.' Although I and the other sitters had no knowledge of this, it turned out that Alfred that weekend had advertised for a rowing boat.

I never failed to be amazed by the range and variety of phenomena at the physical seances I was privileged to witness in those years when physical mediumship seems to have been at its height. Yet another manifestation came my way at Brighton where I had a platform engagement. The lady with whom I was staying (who became another dear friend) mentioned a Mr and Mrs Hodges who regularly conducted direct voice seances privately in their own home. I was becoming quite well known by then, particularly through my transfiguration work, and they asked her to bring me to sit with them next time I came to Brighton.

Mr Hodges was the barber at a public school there. His

wife, who had the care of her elderly mother, stayed at home in their unpretentious little house, identical with so many of its kind: a front room, a middle room leading to the kitchen or scullery and from there a door to the garden. Attendance was strictly by invitation and they only invited two people at a time. On this occasion they did not count my hostess from the Brighton Spritualist Church and there was one other visitor besides myself, a lady who had lost her little son.

It is usual in a physical seance to start the proceedings with singing which in some way helps to raise the vibrations, but with only two sitters this was not possible. Under spiritual direction Mr Hodges had overcome this problem by creating what he called a vibrator. This, so I understood, had an effect on the atmosphere similar to that of singing, helpful to the production of physical phenomena which have to vibrate on a different note from that of the world of matter.

Mr Hodges started with a prayer, very simple and in no way embarrassing, asking that whatever took place would be in accordance with God's will, then he set the vibrator in motion. It made a regular rhythmic sound, rather like the whirring of a piece of machinery, but without being noisy. When the vibrator was in motion we saw a circle of silver light shining in the darkness; quite small, perhaps eight inches across. Then, in the centre of this circle appeared an illuminated silver letter M. The effect was most beautiful and we saw this silver symbol move slowly around the room, first resting gently for a moment on the shoulder of the other sitter before it came to rest gently on mine. I found it quite strange because without touching or any sense of feeling one knew that something was coming.

The M was for Moonstar, Mr Hodges' guide, who then greeted us in a resonant voice, saying how pleased he was to see these friends and that he was bringing as helper a little girl called Rosie who would conduct those who were going to communicate. At this, a delightful childlike voice – in complete contrast to the deep, resonant voice of Moonstar – piped 'Hello, everyone'. A large, illuminated trumpet, usual at such seances, was floating about the room and now the large end pointed towards the other sitter and we heard Rosie speaking through it.

'I have your little boy. He is rather nervous but we have told him that you are here and that although you cannot see him, he will be able to see you.'

This little boy had dashed out from school and gone straight under a bus. Now we heard a quite different childish voice say excitedly, 'Hullo, mummy. It's lovely here. You musn't be worried about me. I didn't feel anything at all. They told me to tell you. I wasn't a bit frightened. I've seen grandma...' and so his voice went on, as if he were writing a letter to his parents.

You can imagine what this meant to his mother. I had a lump in my throat myself when all at once I heard my father's voice with that distinctive intonation. 'Don't be afraid,' he said. 'I just want to touch you.' Very gently I felt his hand – it felt quite solid – on my shoulder, while he spoke to me about what was relevant to my life. Stanley was in the army, and wartime conditions made life extremely hard, but he expressed himself well pleased with what I was doing and told me always to trust my spirit friends.

Although I sat several times with Mr and Mrs Hodges, that

was the only occasion when I received a personal communication. I experienced sprinklings of delightful scent with something of the delicacy of sweet peas and I was present when another memorable reunion with a child took place, a little girl of seven who had been practising ballet steps when her tutu caught fire and she died. Both her parents were present. As the little boy had done, she said reassuring things to comfort them and told them she was going on with her dancing. That again was one of those wonderful evenings of purpose and solace.

It had taken Mr and Mrs Hodges twelve years of dedicated and unremitting practice to develop as they had. During the whole of this time they would never allow anything at all to interfere with their regular night of sitting for development. Even when on holiday they would come back specially for this night and then return to wherever they happened to be staying. Never would they let their attunement be broken and that certainly showed in the quality of all their communication. Sometimes Moonstar would give a little soliloquy, not personal, but always uplifting in its effect. The unexpected was never far away. One evening, Rosie, coming to say goodbye, added, 'I've got a surprise for you.'

'Oh, Rosie,' said Mr Hodges, 'what is that?'

'I'm not telling you,' she said, 'or it wouldn't be a surprise.'

Just as the proceedings always opened with the sight of a silver circlet with the letter M inside, so this symbol would appear when it was time for a session to end and Mr Hodges would say, 'Thank you, Moonstar. We know that we now have to close.'

He would very gradually reduce the vibratory note until it

ceased and then, equally gradually, introduce light into the room. Everything he did was under clear direction from the spirit world. On this particular evening, Rosie having said goodnight and Moonstar having afforded his own parting symbol, we wondered what Rosie could have been referring to. We were a group of five, in an exceedingly small room, and as the light gradually increased, there in the centre we saw a bunch of violets – beautiful violets, looking as if they had just been picked, they even had dew on them. I can still recapture their scent – the old-fashioned strongly scented violets.

I became very good friends with Mr and Mrs Hodges, and with the lady who had introduced me to them. When working in Brighton I would stay with her and she would invite me to stay on for a few days holiday. Normally sitters were invited just once to the seances, although I went two or three times, but we used to meet Mr and Mrs Hodges socially. On one memorable occasion we were all four of us sitting out in one of the Brighton tea gardens. As the waitress came towards us to take our order, 'Oh, no,' we heard Mrs Hodges exclaim, and she seemed extremely put out. We looked at her in surprise, but the waitress had arrived so we turned away to give our order. The waitress departed and again we heard Mrs Hodges say, *'No,* Rosie, please, *no.'*

The table began to shake. Faster and faster it shook, backwards and forwards, while Mrs Hodges' pleas became more anguished. 'Oh, *please,* Rosie, *please,* not *here*.!'

As if to show defiance, in front of our astonished gaze, the table started to walk! It literally moved away from us in full view of everyone at the surrounding tables who stared in amazement, quite stunned, unable to believe their eyes. The waitress, returning with our order of four cream teas on a very large tray, stopped, mouth open, as she saw the table moving towards her, screamed and dropped the tray. China, water, milk, all went crashing to the ground.

Poor Mrs Hodges, scarlet with embarrassment, kept apologising to everyone. 'I'm so sorry,' she kept repeating, 'I'm so sorry.' But of course no-one could understand why she should be sorry. For everyone else this incredible incident had no connection with any particular person. I had always understood that Rosie was inclined to be mischievous but this beat everything.

CHAPTER 11
Hardships and hazards of travelling in wartime. A near-fatal illness.

Being a medium in wartime had its own hazards and on one tour I nearly died. The previous year I had developed bouts of excruciating pain. It used to start deep, deep down in my abdomen, build up to a crescendo and then gradually recede. I would go for months without it, then the pain would come and go again and I would feel all right. When I felt an attack coming on the only way I could stop myself from fainting was to cling on to something solid and lean over it. One of these came on when I was on my way home to Leytonstone after taking a service at Balham. Waiting on the tube station with nothing to lean over I fainted with the pain.

When I came to, a girl in Air Force uniform was standing over me, looking very concerned. After I had recovered somewhat she insisted on accompanying me all the way home. She saw me safely to my door, then left me to make her own long journey back. It was another of those spontaneous acts of kindness I remember from the war and I have always regretted I was never able to thank her properly.

The doctor had at first insisted I must be pregnant but I knew that was out of the question; Stanley was in the army and I had not seen him for months. Then it must be your bladder, the doctor told me, and gave me some medicine. By this time I had suffered ten months of these intermittent pains and looking back I do not know why I left it there. I think it was wartime conditions which made one accept one's own difficulties. At any rate, I did not seek further medical help.

Just three weeks after this attack I was due to leave on a tour of Swindon, Exeter and Bristol. Between them they shared my travelling expenses and the practice was that visiting mediums were put up by each church. At Swindon I was to take a service and give a transfiguration demonstration before travelling on to Exeter. On the day I left London Stanley was due to return to his unit on the Isle of Wight after a few days leave, so he travelled part of the way with me. At Swindon I was hurried to the church where I took the afternoon service and, after being offered only a cup of tea, a transfiguration demonstration in the evening. This finished at about nine o'clock. Overnight accommodation had been arranged for me in a horrible little cafe where I was received by a sternly unsmiling mother and daughter. They did not offer me anything to eat but showed me straight up to an icy room, very bare, with linoleum on the floor and the thinnest blanket I have ever seen. I have never been so cold before or since. I only partially undressed and I remember miserably tucking my feet into my woollen gloves.

When I came down to breakfast, after a very poor night, there were this mother and daughter again, grim-faced like warders in a prison, on the table in front of each a teacup turned upside down. After barely giving me the time to eat the very meagre wartime breakfast, 'Now you can read the cups for us,' they demanded. Quite taken aback, I replied firmly that I never did that sort of thing.

'Oh, but the mediums always read the cups for us when they come,' they said in chorus.

'Well, this one doesn't,' I retorted, 'and if it ever means coming here again I shall refuse the arrangement.'

I will never forget the austerity of that visit. Thankful to put it behind me, on Saturday morning I left Swindon and by about three o'clock in the afternoon arrived at Exeter. This was in 1942, conditions at the time made any journey an ordeal, and Exeter had been badly bombed. There, I was to take the Sunday service and then to demonstrate transfiguration on Monday evening before going on to Bristol the following day. The president of the Exeter church was a keen Spiritualist but his wife loathed everything to do with Spiritualism. It was unfortunate that, because of her husband, visiting mediums were put up in their house. I was met by the wife, whose manner could not have been more unwelcoming. At the house she made it clear that she herself had nothing to do with Spiritualism and that it was only under protest she agreed to put up the mediums her husband invited to his church, after which she showed me to a cold attic room right at the top of the house.

Coming on top of the appalling train journey and the lack of any hospitality in Swindon this rejection shocked me, but there was more to come. After some sort of high tea, this lady informed me that she did not like mediums to spend the evening in the house, adding that they usually went to the theatre. Having little option, I obediently took myself off and sat through an evening performance of *She Stoops to Conquer*.

The production in fact was good, but in view of what happened afterwards I had such a horror of that fateful weekend that I could never bear to see the play after that.

Back at the house, I was at once banished to the attic again, up those three steep flights of steps. On the Sunday I took the afternoon and evening services but all the time with the feeling of being so totally unwelcome in that house that I longed for my work in Exeter to be finished. There was only Monday evening now, on Tuesday I would be off to Bristol.

On Monday morning my reluctant hostess brought tea and toast up to my room, making it clear that she would not have mediums mixing with the rest of the household. I had a book to finish. It was *Random Harvest* I remember, and I had just closed the book, glad of its happy ending, when I felt a familiar pain. 'Oh, no,' I thought, 'Not here, not *here.*'

It became so bad I could hardly bear it. It had never been as bad as this and I knew I needed a doctor. Struggling against the pain and the mounting nausea, I managed to get down those flights of stairs by sitting on each step and lowering myself to the next. When I thought that I could be heard, I called out that I needed a doctor. My hostess answered so promptly she must have been lurking on guard. After saying she would call a doctor, she told me to go back up to bed. Her husband was around because he heard what I said and he took it very badly when I had to tell him I would not be fit to do the evening demonstration. Getting back up those stairs was almost more than I could manage. It took me quarter of an hour. About an hour later the doctor arrived, a huge woman, she must have been six feet tall and weighed about twenty stone. She came puffing up the stairs, poor woman, and said to the lady of the house who had shown her in, 'Why couldn't you have put her somewhere else?'

'Why should I?' this lady replied. 'I think she is pregnant and it is we who have to take the consequences.'

'No,' replied the doctor, 'she is not pregnant but she is extremely ill.' Taking my hand, she turned to me and said in the most kindly way, 'I'm going to get help. You need a surgeon. I'll send an ambulance for you as soon as I possibly can.'

It was well after lunchtime by now. About forty minutes later she returned with a tall elegant man, a surgeon, who very soon confirmed to the doctor that I had a strangulated ovarian cyst. 'Ambulance, immediately,' he said. 'I will operate at once.'

By then it was about four o'clock. At six I was being wheeled into the operating theatre in Exeter hospital, having signed the routine form on which I had filled in my religion as "Spiritualist".

The Matron, a very kind woman whose religion was that of Plymouth Brethren (along with many of the other staff, as I discovered later) was horrified. As I was being wheeled into the operating theatre she came beside the trolley, took hold of my hand, and said, 'My dear, you are desperately ill, I don't think you realise. Are you quite sure you want to be a Spiritualist?'

Of course I just smiled and nodded and the next thing I knew the operation was over. In my ignorance I had expected that after the operation I would be free of that excruciating pain. When I came to in my hospital bed I was lying on my back, my hands at my sides, and in pain from the top of my thighs to my breast bone. True, the pain now was different, but it was nonetheless agonising. Though I did not know this until later, they found an extremely large ovarian cyst, strangulated, their worry all the time that, if they did not remove it before it burst, I could have died of septicemia. I had to have thirty-six stitches.

While I was lying there, feeling miserable and let down, something I had never experienced before lifted me out of my bitter disappointment and almost out of pain. It was as if two enormous warm hands were enfolding my own as they lay at my sides, engulfing them with their warmth. It was a quite physical sensation, as of materialised hands, a heartening gesture of love and reassurance; more than that, it seemed to envelop me in some comforting and uplifted state. I lay there resting in the wonder of it.

The city had been badly bombed, as I knew before I accepted this booking because the church had been partly destroyed and services were held in a hired hall. In London at that time we had hardly had our clothes off for six weeks, night after night in the shelter. There were no military targets in Exeter but they had made an awful mess of the city and people were naturally nervous. We were on the sixth floor and about six o'clock one evening I saw the nurses going round the ward, putting a coil of rope on each bed. I could not think what on earth they were doing and when they came to mine I asked.

'There's an air raid warning,' my nurse said, 'and we have to get the immobile patients down to the shelter. We roll you up in your mattress, tie it securely and send you down a chute to the basement.'

'Oh, no, you don't!' I declared. 'No way would I let myself be tied up in a mattress and sent down a chute.'

'But it's air raid regulations,' she protested.

'I don't care whose regulation it is, I am not going to allow that.'

Some poor soul opposite me had jumped out of bed when she heard that an air raid was expected and promptly fainted. The nurses were running around trying to get her back into bed to secure her in her mattress. The Matron was called to deal with me.

'I don't think you quite realise...' she began, when I retorted, 'You can't force me, and I prefer, if I am going to die, to die in bed. In any case, I shall certainly not die before I am meant to.'

'You realise you will be up here entirely alone?'

I smiled up at her. 'With my religion I am never alone,' I replied, and off she went, another very indignant adherent to the Plymouth Brethren.

I had one friend among the nursing staff who was not a Plymouth Brother but there was one particular day-nurse who was especially antagonistic. After the air raid – it must have been six o'clock in the morning and the night nurses were getting the ward ready for the patients to be brought back – the friendly nurse told me with a smile that the other one had asked scornfully how I had got on, alone on the sixth floor during the bombing.

'Was she afraid?' she demanded. My friend had taken great pleasure in being able to reply, truthfully,

'On the contrary, she was the only one who wasn't. She

had a very comfortable night in bed.'

My extremely reluctant late hostess appeared by my bed one day.

'I hope you don't expect us to pay the consultant's fee,' was almost the first thing she said.

'I don't expect anything from you,' I replied and then she came to the real reason for her visit.

'The hospital have been on at me because they need your bed. They want me to take you as soon as you are well enough to be moved but I have told them that under no circumstances will I have you back.'

'Under no circumstances,' I took some satisfaction in replying, 'would I willingly come back and stay under your roof,' and I watched her walk angrily out of the ward.

Nevertheless, extremely weak as I still was, what was I going to do? This was a real problem. Stanley had gone back to his unit, my mother was at home in London. When the young surgeon came round he brought up the difficulty. Now that it was only a matter of allowing my wound time to heal, the bed was needed for urgent wartime cases.

'Do you not know anyone here?' he asked. I had to say that I did not, that I had never been to Exeter before. 'If I get myself a taxi and get myself to the station,' I asked, 'do you think I could get back to London? My mother would look after me there.'

'Not unless you want to go in a coffin,' he replied. 'You are not fit to stand yet.'

It was true that I had not yet been allowed to get out of bed. 'Oh, well,' he said after a moment, 'we could not discharge you for some days yet in any case. Possibly a week.'

Later, that wonderful lady doctor came to visit. She stood beaming down at me in bed. The consultant she had called in, a very highly regarded surgeon, was a Mr Wayland Smith.

'I wonder if you realise how lucky you are?' she said. 'I caught Mr Wayland Smith by *ten* minutes. If I had been ten minutes later he would have left, and then it would have been too late. When they operated they said you could have gone for just another half an hour – no more – and then nothing, but nothing, would have saved you.'

My poor husband, as I learned afterwards, after leaving me in Swindon on the Friday, had not arrived back at his unit until early on the Sunday morning. Hardly had he reported back when on Monday he was sent for and told that I was dangerously ill. The police offered little hope that he could get to me in time but they thought he ought to try, and he was granted compassionate leave. After another appalling journey – it had meant a day and a night of travelling – he arrived at the hospital in Exeter at six o'clock on the Wednesday morning, when he found me sitting up in bed, though still in considerable pain. 'They told me you were at death's door!' he exclaimed.

'Well, don't look so disappointed,' I said, 'it *was* touch and go. Obviously I was not meant to go yet.' Laughing and coughing were sheer torture and I was still so weak that even talking tired me.

The next day the President of the Spiritualist Church came to see me. After apologising that his wife did not find it convenient to have me, he told me that a member of the church, one who had not been to the Sunday services which I had taken, had offered to have me until I was well enough to travel. A retired nurse, she knew all about the difficulties and her daughter, who was nursing in Bournemouth, happened to be at home on leave. Between them, she had told him, there would be no problem in taking care of me and getting me well enough to travel back to London.

This kindness overwhelmed me. I thought it so wonderful that this lady, who had never even set eyes on me and had no idea what sort of person I was, offered her home and her care so generously. She had four daughters. A son had died in the December 1919 influenza epidemic, which was what had brought her into Spiritualism in the first place. The family virtually adopted me. They nursed me back until I was able to travel and from that was born an enduring friendship.

That whole experience was another milestone in my development. The loving care and kindness I received on leaving hospital entirely wiped out the previous unpleasantness and I could not help reflecting with something like awe on the timing. Grim as it had certainly been, my spirit friends had not only stepped in to save me from disaster, but had conveyed, in a profoundly moving way, their caring and their love as I lay in bed in such pain after coming round from the operation. I began to realise how protected I was on a spiritual level. I saw that always that support had been provided, and with most precise timing, though when one is bogged down in the misery of the physical circumstances it is difficult to register.

One bitter disappointment arising from my illness, however, I had to accept. I had been offered an engagement in

Edinburgh after this tour was over. This invitation had of course delighted me and I had felt truly honoured, because the Edinburgh Psychic College and Library[2] at that time was the most highly thought of in the country and to be invited to demonstrate there meant that you had definitely arrived. At the time I was offered this engagement I had been working professionally from 1939 until 1942 and when I had to write and say that illness would prevent me from coming, it nearly broke my heart.

A famous medium of that time was Helen Hughes, one beloved by the Edinburgh Psychic College. Many years later, when I myself had become established, she said to me, 'It took you only two and a half years to be invited to Edinburgh. It took me eight.'

---

[2] *Now the Edinburgh College of Parapsychology*

CHAPTER 12

Some wartime experiences on tour in Wales. A materialisation seance with Alec Harris.

Touring in wartime meant special hardships for mediums no less than for others whose work involved travelling around the country. While sometimes these were of an unusual kind, others had their funny side, at least in retrospect, and I had my share of both. Some I remember most clearly were while visiting South Wales.

These tours were organised primarily with the object of sharing the expenses as widely as possible with little or no regard for the medium or, at least, certainly not for one as little known as myself in those early days. There were a great many Spiritualist churches in the valleys of South Wales; mining valleys as they were in those days, where the living conditions were very different from now. This was Emlyn Williams country. He owned a theatre in that area and I saw him several times.

I was in fact very young to be a visiting medium and still somewhat naive. Chan had taught me always to present myself as well as possible and then to forget all about myself on the platform. I had never really thought about my appearance in any personal way so it took me by surprise when a guest with us on one occasion, a very prominent official of a national Spiritualist organisation, made a pass at me in the back of the taxi. I expect my rejection then could have been more tactful, but although I may have afterwards learnt how to handle this situation when it did sometimes occur, I always found it utterly distasteful.

The local area president, a dear man, was taking us from Treherbert to Maesteg where I was to give my next demonstration of clairvoyance. He was sitting in front of the taxi with the driver, presumably unaware of what was going on in the back. When we arrived he invited the driver to come to the meeting, because of course, he was engaged to wait for us. I did not appreciate how lucky we were to be making that journey in a taxi. At one place I was told that we had missed the bus to the next engagement and would have to walk. I certainly had not reckoned on walking up a mountainside carrying my own luggage. No-one offered to help, although I had quite a bit of equipment with me. Transfiguration is ectoplasmic and I carried a special garment for this, in order to conserve the energy, and a cap to cover my hair. Added to this was a lamp with a red bulb, together with its special lamp stand. The tour was quite successful but the shocks were not over. On the fourth night – I have forgotten which of the valley towns it was – the loo was at the end of a long garden. Seeing the dismay with which I received this information, my hostess told me proudly how lucky I was.

'They have only just put that in,' she said. 'Until a month ago we had to go up the mountain.'

At another of these towns – it may have been Ystalyfera – I was asked if my guides would address the audience in

Welsh. They did not understand when I explained that the guides had to use *my* brain and *my* vocabulary; and although the demonstration could not be called a failure, it had a flat, empty feeling. There was another place on this tour where I felt the same dampening effect.

It is hard, looking back, to realise how very naive I was in those days. As I worked entirely in trance, I was not conscious of what went on around me nor of how my mediumship was received and while I was often upset by people's comments, in another way I was very detached.

I can laugh, in retrospect, at what happened in Port Talbot, but at the time it was very hard to take. The previous evening's engagement had been in Neath and I arrived in Port Talbot at about half past eleven, to be met by a large, buxom lady, very friendly and most welcoming in her manner. She took me to her house, showed me into a very pleasant room with a big double bed, and said that lunch would be ready as soon as I had unpacked.

Downstairs my place was laid at a fair-sized table and as soon as I sat down, out from another door – presumably the kitchen – came a very appetising plate of fish and chips. Still alone at the table, I ate this with enjoyment, leaving the bones and discarded bits of skin quite neatly on the side. When I had finished, a little boy of about ten came in, said a friendly 'Hello' and took my plate away; only to return with a fresh portion of fish and chips, but with all my discarded bits on the side of the plate, to which he added his own bits of bone and skin. To my utter amazement, this happened four times. Four different people came in, picked up the plate, took it to the kitchen and came back with a fresh portion of fish and chips while the discarded bits piled up on the side.

I was equally fascinated and puzzled by this. Then I did the worst possible thing.

After I had eaten I was brought a cup of tea. Again, I enjoyed this, and when I had finished, I took the empty cup into the kitchen which was just at my elbow, opening out of the room where we had been eating. But in the doorway I stood, shocked and appalled, when I saw the unbelievably dirty state of the kitchen and everything in it. I would not have washed floors with the tea towels hanging there. Seeing that terrible squalor I realised why everyone used the same plate; it was probably the only one that had been washed (though this still did not explain the accumulation of the discarded bits). They might well have had no running water, I thought, remembering the newly-installed sanitary arrangements at the end of that back garden, but whatever the reason, I knew I could take nothing more which came out of that kitchen, not even a cup of tea. I would have to survive fasting. In spite of this I was anxious not to hurt the lady of the house, a widow; she was such a nice person.

The transfiguration seance that evening was particularly successful, there was a great deal of power in the room and all those present were most responsive and helpful. Coming back to normal consciousness after a powerful demonstration was always difficult and that night I was extremely tired. Once in bed I lay there, unable to sleep and wondering how I would manage to refuse any breakfast.

Suddenly I was no longer in bed, I was floating round the room, faster and faster, as if driven by a whirlwind. Never had I experienced anything like it – although I have since, after my bladder operation when I had a similar, rather frightening experience. When I had deliberately learnt to leave my body I had achieved it gradually, step by step, and I knew what I was doing. But this happened quite out of the blue. I was being chased round and round the room, up near the ceiling, and I could not even see my body lying on the bed.

'Chan! Help me!' I cried, and suddenly I was lying in bed, almost winded. I was terribly out of breath, as if I had been running.

Chan explained to me afterwards that this was due to vibratory adjustment, toning down again to the slower rhythms of my body. It must have taken ten minutes, I had terrible palpitations until it passed off and sheer exhaustion sent me to sleep.

In the morning I asked my hostess if she was aware of the psychic activity in that room and described my experience. She laughed, saying it was her own room and that she had been told she had an enormous amount of psychic power.

'I suppose you tuned in to that,' she commented. 'I have never been whizzed around as you describe but I have felt as if I were on a roundabout, my head whirling – not giddy, but nothing stands still.'

In my vulnerable state last night I had been wide open to these energies.

She was such a nice woman, and so were her family, a daughter employed in the steelworks and the little boy; all so friendly and welcoming.

I used to do one tour a year in Wales and I remember them as being on the whole very pleasant and very successful. There was one occasion however which would have given rise to a clash of loyalties had I not been quite clear in my own mind that I had dedicated myself to Chan's service. I was touring Wales when Stanley was given leave prior to being sent to France. He felt I should cancel and come home. He took it very badly when I reminded him that, when Chan asked if I were ready to put this work before anything, we had sworn that we were.

'But Chan didn't mean *that*,' protested Stanley. 'There wasn't a war on then.' But I had given my word and for me that was that.

It was on a tour in Wales that I was privileged to attend the most extraordinary demonstration of physical phenomena I have ever witnessed. I had an engagement in Cardiff and my host invited me afterwards to go with him and his wife to a materialisation seance with Alec Harris, later an extremely famous materialisation medium but then practically unknown. He was also most reluctant about his extraordinary gift. If I remember rightly, he was an engineer in normal life. His wife played the violin in a theatre orchestra so it was not until she returned after the evening performance that the seances could start. These took place in a small upstairs room in which a cabinet had been arranged by hanging blackout curtains across one corner. In contrast to those of Helen Duncan, these curtains remained open and the medium was fully visible the whole time. Like her, he was stripped and searched beforehand and came back in a very loose tunic and trousers of blackout material. I sat with my host and Mrs Harris, beside me their son David, aged about twelve. Across the room were three rows of sitters, perhaps some twenty people in all. A central red light provided illumination.

It was customary for the seances to start with a solo from David. In his very beautiful choirboy's voice he sang *The Lord is My Shepherd*. Meanwhile, fully visible to us all, Alec went into trance and just as the glorious notes of the last verse died away, the curtains billowed very slightly, as if stirred by a breeze.

With Helen Duncan, materialisations came gradually. You could see the flow of the ectoplasm; it came out in a ribbon before expanding into a form. With Alec it was different. There was just a slight tremor of the curtains and there before your eyes was a form. One moment there was nothing and the next moment he was there, and we could still see Alec sitting in the cabinet, apparently quite unchanged. The materialised figure, Alec's guide, whose name also was David, had a long grey beard. He stepped out and in a very Welsh voice thanked little David for his singing which, he said, had done much to build up the power, before very courteously greeting everyone. Then, before addressing me directly, he asked the sitters across the room if they would excuse him for a moment.

'Your spirit friends are extremely pleased that you are here this evening,' he said, turning to me, 'but they do not intend to manifest for you. There are so many here who need the consolation of conviction of survival, but you have no such need. I have been asked to give you their love, to say that they are participating this evening, helping in any way they can, and that they are most grateful for the opportunities you afford them to bring comfort and enlightenment to the bereaved.' Then he turned to Mrs Harris. 'May I, madam, have your permission to take one of these roses out of your vase and, on behalf of her spirit friends, give this to this lady?' As he handed me the flower I took it by the stem.

As I have explained, I cannot bear to be touched in these situations and with my mind I made my usual plea, whereupon the figure said, 'My dear, would you shake hands with me?' Thus forewarned I felt no reluctance to take his hand. To my astonishment it was the tiny hand of a child of five. In my mind – I said nothing out loud – but in my mind I said to myself, 'This is a child's hand.' *Instantly* he smiled and said, 'Nobody wants to see hands, it is faces they are interested in, and if we make the hands a little smaller it conserves the power for that more important feature.' Then, giving a little chuckle, he turned from me and addressed the rows of sitters across the room. 'I am now going to send those loved ones to you who will try to manifest tonight. It is most important that you answer, because your contact is the supporting rod of energy that will maintain the materialised form.'

Alec's guide was very much more informative than Albert and there was not that slight feeling of being patronised. I never felt comfortable with Albert but David took time to explain the procedure; he made you really glad to be there and anxious to help in any way you could. Now he explained, 'Before we begin these proceedings we need to lighten the atmosphere. My hostess is a musician but she has already been working this evening at the theatre. We have our own methods of lightening the atmosphere, which is all that music does; it breaks down the tension inevitably arising when people are in an unknown situation. I shall depart and a little light-hearted creature will take my place.'

There was something like a flash, a "whoosh..." into the

curtain and, before we had time to realise it, David was no longer there and in his place was a little girl. She was fully formed, with dark skin and a mass of curly black hair, clothed not in loose draperies but in a whitish-pink dress with a frill on the skirt, which came just to her knees. Nothing could have been more different from the materialised form of Alec's guide than this little girl perched on the lap of the medium, whom we could see quite clearly sitting with his head down and his arms loosely folded as if asleep.

'I love him very much,' she said and gave him a kiss but with no response from him; he was quite unaware. 'I know he is asleep,' she went on, 'but his other bit – his spirit bit – *he* knows I have kissed him.' Then she explained, 'I am here to tell you who is coming. David tells me what to do but I am the conductor.' And she threw back her head importantly, shaking her mop of curly hair. She had the most lovely eyes and very dainty features.

'You won't see me,' she continued. 'You will only hear my voice because you people want to see bodies, and if they have bodies I can't have mine, but I will tell you what to do. The first person who wants to come is another little girl.'

With that, Topsy was gone and we heard her voice asking if there was someone who had a little girl called Dorothy. 'Speak up,' she said. 'This is where you must speak up.' From towards the back of the room a voice acknowledged a daughter named Dorothy. 'Go on, Dolly,' we heard Topsy's voice, 'your mother is here.' And there before us was a white child with her hair done in ringlets and wearing a very ordinary child's dress and white socks and shoes. She greeted her mother and we heard Topsy's voice, 'Come on, answer her, answer her.' The mother, quite overwhelmed and speechless with emotion, at last managed, 'Oh, Dorothy, it's lovely to see you!'

'Look!' said this lovely little being, pointing to her ringlets. 'I don't have to have these tied up in rags, hurting and pulling my hair. They come like this.' Both parents were in tears. It was these trivial but evidential details which carried conviction, as when an older man who had been killed in an accident materialised in overalls and we could even see the dust on them.

All this time we did not see Topsy but heard her voice. Then followed the most spectacular episode I have ever experienced in my life. Topsy started by asking, 'Who is it here who does a lot of what they call healing?' Three of the sitters spoke up.

'Well, I don't know,' said Topsy. 'I don't know which one of you he wants, but there is a great, big Indian here – oh, he *is* a big man, so you will really have to help with this. All you people who are healers, just think about healing and send your thoughts to help him make up the extra body.'

To the stunned amazement of us all, suddenly before us was a North American Indian at least seven feet tall, olive-skinned with sharply defined features, beaked nose and very firm mouth, clothed in a white leather suit with fringed edges. Two enormous plaits of hair hung down in front of him. We were all dumbstruck. He stood looking around him in a very imperious way. 'He wants to find his medium,' we heard Topsy say. Someone asked his name, at which Topsy apparently experienced difficulty because she did not reply. Several people then asked the same at which the Indian figure jumped up and down with frustration and then appeared to mutter something which nobody could understand. An impasse seemed to have been reached when suddenly he turned to the mantlepiece where a carafe of water and a glass had been placed. He carefully poured the water into the glass, then turning back, he gently poured the water onto the floor.

'Ah!' exclaimed a lady sitting directly in front of him, 'You are Running Water,' whereupon he bent and embraced this lady.

Now this episode raises all sorts of questions, not least, why did he not know her? As far as I can understand, those in spirit do not identify the physical body because their awareness is of the spirit. As soon as the healer acknowledged him he focussed on her spirit and so was able to recognise her. He then held out his plaits and we heard Topsy say that he wanted those in the back row to take hold of them. To our amazement, they stretched across to where two sitters in the back row picked up the ends, and he ran his hands along them. Then, through Topsy, he said he wanted by this to convey to his medium the power he was directing to her, and he gave some instructions for a particular case she was trying to help.

Then, again with the same suddenness, he was no longer there. In his place was a rather hunched old lady. All this time, Alec continued to be visible in his cubicle; we could see that he had not moved. She had a wrinkled face with deep lines down from the mouth suggesting a bad temper. In a very querulous voice with a strong Welsh accent, she said, 'My daughter is here.' As a voice answered her, this old lady trod in the water which Running Water had poured on the floor. 'I think it's disgusting,' she remarked, looking down at this. 'People are so slovenly. Why don't they wipe up these messes?' As the embarrassed daughter tried to explain, her mother interrupted. 'I don't care who it was, they shouldn't have left it like this.'

The daughter tried again. 'I'm so pleased to see you, mother.'

'Are you?' demanded the old lady crossly, and went on to criticise her daughter for all the things she was doing wrongly at home. It became very clear to us all that just being in the spirit world and not in a physical body did not, in itself, improve the character.

It was about eleven o'clock when the seance actually started. The materialisations continued, all with personal evidential details, until two o'clock in the morning, everyone staggered by the wonder of it all. Alec's guide, David, had exuded a special quality, making us feel that we were indeed loved.

It was July. The house, some way out of Cardiff, stood on a hill overlooking the town; in the distance we could see the surrounding hills. I looked up at the sky and it seemed that literally millions of stars were shining down on me. I stood there quietly for a while, wrapped in the wonder of it all, and it came to me how difficult – how impossible – it must be for people to believe such things could really happen. I had only just come from witnessing them, but even I could hardly believe that they had actually taken place.

I realised now more clearly what Chan had meant when he said I needed to understand the difficulty people had when they started to investigate and how important it was for me to be able to say that I *knew* these things were true, that I had seen them for myself.

I was still holding the rose that David had picked out of a vase and given to me. I treasured this, of course I did, but with no idea then of the extraordinary sequel. Carefully wrapped in damp tissue, I took it home and put it in water. When the mass of violets materialised at the end of an evening in the Hodges' circle in Brighton, we each took some home. Mine had lasted for a few days, as any violets would, so every day I expected the rose to show signs of fading. Days went by, then weeks. Each morning I looked at it in amazement. That flower lasted for three months with no sign of withering or decay until, one morning in September, I came down and there was no flower. No dead leaves or dead bloom, no stem – nothing in the clear water but around the base of the vase was a circle of ash, like cigarette ash.

I can only think that when Alec's guide held it in his hands before presenting it to me he impregnated it with some sort of spiritual energy, and that because of the faster frequency of that energy it did not go through the stages of physical decay but turned immediately to dust – the cancellation of the physical level. Whenever I am feeling a bit down or uncertain, wondering at some low moment whether I might not be deluding myself, I go back to that memorable night. With all due respect to Helen Duncan and the others who played their part in my education, for me, that night with Alec Harris was the crown of everything that was convincing.

CHAPTER 13

Some other remarkable mediums; Helen Hughes and Hannah Swaffer. Ivy's mother dies. Her husband is invalided out of the army. Ivy's mediumship begins to gain recognition and she is invited to work at The Spiritualist Association of Great Britain. Janet comes into her life

This was an era of astonishing physical phenomena, as the latter part of the previous century had been. The wonder of these was essentially physical, but the spiritual note – an unmistakable spiritual quality – which made itself felt through the mental mediumship of some outstanding mediums, was just as convincing, over and above the accuracy of the evidence. Helen Hughes was one of those who brought conviction in this way.

She won my heart the first time I ever saw her, at a Spiritualists' National Union Conference at Kingsway Hall. The huge hall was packed in every possible space. I was fortunate enough to be sitting at the front of the gallery with a clear view of all the proceedings. The main speaker was Hannan Swaffer, a famous journalist of his day, well known for his advocacy of psychic matters and for his unfailingly controversial style. A private circle met in his house, those invited being sworn not to reveal the identity of the medium. Not for many years did it become known that this was Maurice Barbanell, the medium for Silver Birch, in professional life the editor of *Psychic News*. Hannan Swaffer was a very tall, somewhat intimidating man with iron grey hair and a very long and prominent jaw. He always wore a black suit, a black coat fastened around the throat and, in the street, a wide brimmed black felt hat. Caricaturists of the day had no difficulty at all in depicting him.

In those days mediumship was not legal; mediums were grouped with rogues and vagabonds under the Vagrancy Act of 1824, and Hannan Swaffer, through his column and his lectures, campaigned to get it legalised. This occasion was no exception. Roundly denouncing sceptics – although what he said was true – he seemed to hurl the words at you belligerently and some of his statements were positively venomous. At the end of his lecture the feeling in the hall among that huge audience was far from harmonious.

When at last he sat down, Helen Hughes came on; quite tiny, dressed all in black and with wispy, baby hair, she still looked charming. As soon as she appeared it was as if the whole atmosphere came to life with sparks of electricity. This tiny figure walked onto that huge stage – it really was huge, with a grand piano some way behind her – and said quietly, 'I wonder, friends, do you know that lovely hymn "When peace like a river ascendeth our souls"?' Unaccompanied we all spontaneously burst into singing and when we stopped it was indeed as if there had been a storm and you could feel the waters abating, giving place to a wonderful silent harmony.

Her mediumship was equally impressive, so accurate and so gentle. With no hesitation at all she picked out the recipient of each communication, she knew exactly where they were sitting in that huge assembly. Hers was a quality of mediumship I had not met before, it was quite superb.

To my great joy, I came to know her later. She often demonstrated in Edinburgh and was always offered the hospitality of the Psychic College, even though she might be appearing elsewhere in the city, and on my visits we overlapped from time to time. She had a brother who used to accompany her; I think he was a miner who had been invalided out and she took care of him. They were extremely poor. In her early days in Newcastle she did not even have a dress to appear in so her friends had a whip-round and bought one for her. She never lost a true humility, side by side with the wonderful spiritual note of her mediumship.

Once when I was working in Edinburgh, I had breakfast with Helen and her brother on Sunday and later went into the church where she was to demonstrate that morning. I could see that the man sitting next to me was in a state of great distress and we were soon in conversation.

'I feel such a fool being here,' he said, 'but I have just heard that my son in the RAF is missing, presumed dead.' Overcome with emotion, he went on. 'The last letter he sent said "I'm coming home on leave, Dad, and I should be with you on Sunday" – that's today – ' and his eyes filled with tears, 'I'm just grasping at straws, I suppose, I don't really believe in this.' My heart went out to the poor man in his distress.

At the end of the session Helen identified the man beside me and gave the last message. 'I have your son here,' she said. 'His name is Alan. He tells me to say, if only he could have stopped that letter. He knew how much it would hurt, how much it would increase your pain. And he goes on, "but I told you, Dad, I would have been home today, and here I am".'

She could not possibly have known about this letter. That

clinched it for Alan's father.

My first public engagement had been in 1939 and it was during the war years that I grew to be better known and fairly constantly in demand. Frequently my engagements took me away from home and these clashed with times when Stanley came home on leave. My mother kept house and looked after the children, while I – as always in my life after I had committed myself – put my mediumship first. I did not feel Stanley had cause for complaint because he had made the same promise I had, though without realising what it might mean in the future. Stanley did not feel about this as I did.

'What sacrifices?' he had asked, and when Chan told us that if we agreed to commit ourselves the work would take precedence over our other arrangements he had never envisaged what it might mean in wartime. But I had no doubts and this caused a rift in our marriage.

By the end of the war my mother's health was failing. She had bronchial asthma, I was away a great deal, and the difficulties of rationing and other day-to-day problems were becoming even more severe. When the time came for all the children who had been evacuated to return home, we decided, very reluctantly, that my mother was not fit enough to look after Sally again. She did not want to leave Wales, she had been so happy there, and one aspect of her return to Lowestoft makes me very sad to think about now, although I did not know it at the time.

When Sally was a baby and Dolly used to visit us each week, Sally knew very well that Dolly was her mother. After some years in Wales, however, never seeing Dolly (I did manage to visit her there), she became confused and thought of me as her mother, so it was all the more hurtful when, at the age of only five or six, she was sent to another place under the impression that I, her mother, was not willing to have her back. Why Dolly, who had herself returned to Lowestoft, never explained the situation, I cannot imagine. When Sally grew older I kept in touch with her by letter and something I wrote prompted her to ask who her real mother was. It made me very sad to realise then what she had thought and I did all in my power to assure her of my love and that it was not through any lack of it that we were unable to look after her at the time she had to leave Wales. We have remained friends ever since. Philip came with me to see her married to an extremely nice man but by the irony of fate Sally, who longed for a baby, was unable to have one, while her mother had conceived all too easily. I have always thought of Sally as part of our family and from time to time have been to see her in Norwich where she lives. Dolly died in a nursing home just a few weeks before her ninetieth birthday.

My mother died in 1946 after only a few days' illness. I was sitting with her and observed something wonderful. At the moment she died I *saw* the spirit leave her body, almost like a puff of smoke, but indescribable. It was a most remarkable experience. I have never forgotten what I saw then, though I have never seen it again.

In later life it was a great sadness to me that I never really knew my mother in the sense of being close to her. She worked so hard – and for a pittance in those days – in order to support us that we had so little time together. I never knew family life and this lack was why my brother, two years older and running wild in the streets after school hours, fell in with undesirable company. My mother thought she was acting in his best interests when she agreed that he would be better cared for in a home. Over the years we lost touch and it was not until shortly before he died that, making contact with him again, I learned the sad truth that he had thought his mother did not love him and wanted to be rid of him. The reverse was true, she loved my brother more than me, but in those days we were even more guilty than we are now of not telling children enough.

Meanwhile, Stanley's health too, had been deteriorating, and in 1946, the year my mother died, he was invalided out of the army. Just how sensitive Stanley was I realise more clearly now. He was also an extraordinarily kind man. One day he brought home the three children of a man he knew at work in Smithfield because their mother was in hospital, taking on a full share of the work entailed. He would bath them every night and make sure they had clean clothes for the next day; he helped me in every way. He had such a generous spontaneity about him, army life must have put him under a terrible strain. He suffered a nervous breakdown and after a while went into a hospital not far from Eastbourne where his mother lived. Philip was in the Air Force and Derek, articled to a chartered accountant, obtained a transfer to Eastbourne to be near his father. So, although my mother had been keeping house and taking off my shoulders all domestic cares, these were not pressing now.

Although my mediumship was my major concern it was no help financially. Half a crown – two shillings and sixpence (twelve and a half pence in today's money) – was the normal fee for taking a service or a demonstration, so I always had to work. My clerical job at Sainsburys was from 8.30 am until 1 pm but as I was undertaking Sunday evening services at churches quite far afield, I often had to plead sick as my excuse for being late on Monday mornings. Not unnaturally, my employers after a while found this unacceptable. Suggesting that I should find something more suitable to my health, they gave me a week's notice. I was devastated. How was I going to pay the mortgage? I was never in debt, I had a horror of it. Not knowing what else to do, I put up a plea to my spirit friends:

'If you want me to go on working for you, you must find me a job.'

On my last Friday a customer whom I knew by sight happened to stop and speak to me and in the course of conversation I mentioned that I was leaving that day.

'Oh,' she said, 'my husband works at Berrys Pianos and I know they need a new clerk.' I applied and was engaged to start work the following Monday. Above all, the hours were flexible. So long as the work was done I could arrange them to suit myself, so no more problems with Monday mornings.

One Monday evening, it was the 21st March 1950, Derek, who was living with his grandmother in Eastbourne, came to tell me that Stanley had died during the night. I had been with him the previous day. He hated being in hospital and I had told him he could come home and I would do my best to look after him, while secretly wondering how I could possibly manage to do that. Stanley's life had been a sad one and there had seemed nothing in it for him to look forward to, so for him

I could not truly grieve.

It was only when I came to reflect on my life that I fully realised the key role in my life's work which Stanley had played. I like to think that after his passing he became aware of his unique and indispensable contribution to the pattern of my development which seemed to have been laid down from the moment I was born, and possibly before. I would become aware of Stanley's loving and supportive presence around me at times of crisis in my life. In our tiny back garden we had planted a lilac tree and lilac became a symbol to me of a special kind of happiness. For his funeral, which took place in Eastbourne, I asked for one wreath to be placed on his coffin, stipulating that it must have lilac in it. When the flowers arrived with no lilac, I refused to accept them. My mother-in-law was horrified and the florists insisted there was no lilac to be had. But I had seen some in a shop window when walking from the station and in due course the wreath came back with one spray of white lilac.

One year it so happened that on my birthday I was ill in hospital, feeling very sorry for myself, when a card was delivered with a picture of lilac and a note inside. The writer, a woman I did not know but who had seen me demonstrate, explained that she was walking past a stationer's shop when "some inner force" impelled her to go inside and buy the card with the lilac on it.

Philip was living at home again, having been invalided out of the RAF. He suffered from epilepsy but not too severely; it would be six months or so between each attack. Then he had a terrifyingly severe one which would have proved fatal had I not been at home and managed to summon help. As my engagements regularly took me away, Derek came to the rescue and arranged to be transferred back to London so that he could live at home with Philip. There were times when I set out for an engagement wondering if I would find Philip alive on my return. Once there, however, the rigid discipline which Chan had instilled in me took over and I was able to maintain my standard on the platform. Altogether that was an extremely difficult time for me, domestically, emotionally and mediumistically. After that crisis Philip did not have another attack for two years during which time he met his future wife, Mary (who incidentally happened to be a nurse). Chan has explained epilepsy as misplaced psychic energy which gets out of control and distorts what he calls the partnership with the physical energy.

The time came for Derek to take his final examinations. When the results were announced it was someone at work who excitedly waved a copy of *The Times* in front of me with Derek's name among the first three in the whole country. Too modest to tell me this himself, when he telephoned he just said he had passed.

At that time the acknowledged centre of excellence for mediumship was the Marylebone Spiritualist Association (soon to be renamed The Spiritualist Association of Great Britain) and to work there as a medium was public recognition that one had arrived. In charge was Ralph Rossiter who had repeatedly asked me to write in for an audition, then the standard method of acceptance. Much as I longed to work there, I had long ago promised Chan that I would never, ever ask for work, so on each occasion I had to tell Ralph Rossiter this and each time the matter was dropped.

Standards were stricter in those days and when applying for the Diploma of the Spiritualists' National Union one had to provide a list of all one's public engagements for the next two years, so that the SNU representatives could assess one's performance on any occasion without the knowledge of the medium. I had gained an SNU Diploma in this way and was invited to speak at their annual May Meeting in Kingsway Hall. If I remember correctly, this would have been around 1950.

Those with me on the platform were extremely well-known, or became so later, notably Gordon Higginson who slipped in at the last minute and fell into the chair next to mine in a most painful state of nerves. He was literally trembling. When his turn came he was, as always, marvellous; he was exceptionally factual in his clairvoyance. That was the beginning of a lasting friendship.

At a class I was taking I had been putting Chan's methods into practice and I thought this would be a good subject for this meeting so I talked about the need for individualising, for not working as a group all the time. After I had spoken, one of those on the platform, he was Musical Director of the Salvation Army, looked across at me,

'I hope you won't misunderstand me, Mrs Northage,' he said, 'but you are the first clairvoyant with whom I am entirely comfortable. I felt that although you are using a different approach, we are on the same path.'

I found that immensely reassuring. My strict training had taught me to be precise; either it was there or not. But Chan also taught me the importance of tact. There are ways of conveying truth, above all when giving messages at public demonstrations. It was quite an honour for me to be on that distinguished platform and to meet some who later became my friends. Furthermore, although I did not know it at the time, that May Meeting was the indirect cause of the most important meeting of the second half of my life. As I was leaving, Ralph Rossiter was waiting to ask me if I would come to the SAGB for a trial.

'Are you inviting me?' I asked. When he replied that he was, this was all I needed. Some time after this he asked if I would take over the class of Winifred Ragless who was leaving in two week's time. I jumped at this and asked to sit in at her last class to see something of her procedure, knowing that I would have to introduce changes. My training methods, which had been taught to me by Chan, were very different from those of most mediums but under his direction I hoped to bring about the change gently. For Winifred's final class I was sitting beside her. I had naturally expected her to introduce me as their new teacher. However, she said nothing at all and the class broke up and dispersed. The following week, when I appeared in charge of the class, they were stunned.

'But didn't Winifred tell you?' I asked.

'No,' they almost shouted, and then it all came out. Winifred had been in the habit of inviting friends to attend her class and she gave them all a good deal of her attention. The regular students who had paid their course fees naturally resented this and had taken me for another hanger-on.

From the beginning I felt a certain antagonism, not only from the class as a whole but in particular from a student who had always sat on Winifred's left and now sat on mine. I was very conscious of not exactly dislike, she was too tolerant and honest for that, but of a definite lack of cooperation, almost disapproval, emanating from her. Her name was Janet and she, like the others, had been used to the easy-going ways of this circle up until then and here I was changing all that with my insistence on preparation and the need to know your psychic mechanism and how to use it.

For some time I had, as usual, been grossly overworking. I had been invited back to Chelmsford, in Essex, to give classes again in addition to my regular midweek and Sunday services there and at other churches, all of which entailed a fair amount of travelling, while of course my daily work at Berrys had to be dealt with, even though I could choose my hours. The boys were living at home at this time and as well as the much heavier domestic load, I had piles of dirty shirts each week to wash and iron. No easycare in those days and one washed them in the public washing-house. Sometimes on a Friday it was two o'clock in the morning before I finished. On Saturday I would be occupied with the preparations for going away because each weekend I would be off to Brighton or elsewhere around the country, returning home on Monday morning to start work at Berrys in the afternoon. It was a pretty exhausting programme. We lived in Leytonstone but the station at Leyton was a bit nearer and I can remember times when I had no recollection of getting from the station to my front door, just passing out when I got there. At other times I would find myself on the floor in my bedroom having been violently sick.

I got no warning of these attacks, one of which hit me at

the end of a session when the class was coming back to normal awareness. Just at that moment when I was losing consciousness I felt from Janet something like a streak of lightning come straight into my solar plexus as she caught me so that I did not fall to the ground. It was almost like sheet lightning, a triangular white light. It seems hardly credible to relate, but it made a noise like a rush of air. My only comparison is an experience with Stanley many years before. He and I were a few rows back in a church with a man sitting directly in front of me when, from the medium on the platform to this man, with a kind of rushing sound, came a similar white streak of light.

Janet has since told me that she knew nothing of this but it changed my whole attitude towards her. Having decided I must tell her that my class was not the right one for her, I had been going to do so that evening. However, when I had recovered sufficiently Janet insisted on taking me home. Next day, she telephoned to enquire how I was and was horrified to learn that such blackouts were regular occurrences at that time. I think it had been introduced into her consciousness that she had been chosen to look after me, because from then on she did all she could to take care of me. Although she lived in Brixton and I in Leytonstone she would make a point of visiting me; she would find out where my Sunday engagements were and come to that church so that, if needed, she could take me home.

As everyone who knows me is aware, Janet's partnership and unfailing, dedicated support have been the foundation on which my work has since been built. At an early sitting with Chan he told her she had two courses open to her: she could establish her own individual mediumship or she could become my helper and protector, but not both. In her generosity of spirit, and feeling I really needed her, she elected to look after me. She has said since that if she had realised what she was in for, she would never have entertained the idea! But I know she does not mean that and it has been a wonderful partnership. Temperamentally, we are quite unalike, sometimes irritating each other, but at a deep level we belong together in inseparable spiritual unity. There is no barrier between us and looking back on that peculiar streak of light I have wondered if it signified a reconnection, if we have been together before.

Janet was living alone in Brixton at that time. Derek, after qualifying, went to do his National Service, so when Philip and Mary married, I moved upstairs and let them have the ground floor of my house. Some time after that it seemed sensible for me to go and live with Janet and over the years, though moving as we felt inclined, we have made our home together ever since.

CHAPTER 14

Ivy declared Medium of the Year at Psychic News annual dinner.

Some years previously, when first asked if I would take a development class, I blithely agreed, until Chan pulled me up short. 'You know nothing about how to conduct a circle,' he told me bluntly. At that time I had been doing platform work with his approval for about eight years, so I was taken aback. 'Do you want to learn to teach?' he asked me. When I assured him that I did, he agreed to undertake my training. It took a further two years before he pronounced me qualified to teach. His methods were different from those of many mediums and over the years I have been made very aware of this.

When Ralph Rossiter first invited me to work at the Spiritualist Association of Great Britain, at a time of great change and expansion after the move to Belgrave Square, he did not know the range of my capacity and it was only gradually that I established myself there. I was taking Winifred Ragless's class, but was I capable of taking Sunday services or of giving lectures? I had sometimes been invited to give the Sunday address and, to try me out, Ralph asked me to give a series of four Chan lectures. As always, I put this to Chan. He was quite agreeable, but when I asked about preparation, 'What preparation?' he said. 'I am doing this, not you.'

Unknown to me at that time, there were always one or two Council members in the audience to vet the performance of untried lecturers or mediums. They were impressed and wrote very favourably of these lectures in the house journal; there were no recordings at that time. As a result I was asked to take another class, this time of my own choosing, though as yet there was no mention of my name in the monthly syllabus. Ralph would scour the country in search of talent and promising mediums would be asked to write in. If they were accepted, it would be for a two-year probationary period. I think standards were higher in those days, perhaps because of what was demanded by those responsible for organising mediumship.

At the Sunday services there was always a double platform, one medium giving the address and another the clairvoyance. I sometimes felt not exactly a barrier but a slight constraint between myself and other mediums, which I put down to the extremely disciplined way in which I had developed under Chan's sole tuition. For instance, I had a great respect and admiration for Ursula Roberts, but she was not really my kind of person and something of this was reflected in the fact that quite tacitly we seemed to agree to differ. Then, one year, we found ourselves together at a Greater World Study Course at Scarborough. I was on the platform to give clairvoyance while her main contribution was healing through her very well-loved guide, Ramadhan.

After I had been home about three weeks, to my

amazement, I received a letter from Ursula, saying how much she had appreciated working with me and how much she had admired the way I handled my particular field. I felt this to be an acknowledgement that she, too, had felt some kind of barrier and of course I responded, expressing my very sincere admiration for her work. Not long after that we found ourselves together at Bristol, our mutual respect creating genuine harmony on the platform.

Later I heard her recount the misfortunes of her early life when she had been afflicted with polio. I had previously had no idea of this nor of all that had gone into overcoming this misfortune, her fortitude and her courage, something I always admire. I don't think courage means standing up to the lion but bravely facing life and dealing with it, even when you feel you have not the ability or the guts to do so. Ursula spent seven years of her early life in hospital, and it was when I learnt of her courage through this time that my barriers simply melted away. And when mine did, something in her also opened up to me.

Chan's teaching methods, as I have said, were in many ways quite different from the less demanding practices of most development circles, not only in regard to the extremely strict discipline he insisted on, but as he had explained to me, in the need to treat each member separately. Each needed more individual attention and more individual practice than was normally afforded in such circles if students were to develop in the way best suited to their particular gift. As everyone who is familiar with my work knows, teaching became for me perhaps the most important part of my work and to some extent the main focus of my energy, though I still carried out engagements all over the country to take services or demonstrations of clairvoyance.

As well as my teaching work at the S.A.G.B., I had been asked to take classes at Brentwood again and these led to my being asked if I would take a class in Chelmsford, all of which entailed rather more travelling, and I began to feel that perhaps I should try to set up my own school of mediumship.

This was a bigger undertaking than I had bargained for and, looking back, I can see why it did not prove to be the right thing for me.

My particular relationship with Chan set me apart. I was not a free agent in the way many other mediums were, and this showed itself in what brought my school of mediumship to an end. However, around that time I met someone from among my students at the S.A.G.B. who shared my enthusiasm, and together we set up and launched a school of mediumship which became known by word of mouth and met with considerable success. In the very early 1970's – it may have been 1971 or 1972 – I took a party of some sixty of our students to the annual dinner organised by *Psychic News*. To my utter amazement, when the announcement was made, I was named as Medium of the Year for, it was stated, my contribution to the development of mediumship. Janet was with me, of course, and also my brother who had very recently lost his wife. That was my first public commendation and it was a wonderful and gratifying surprise.

With the success of the school the expenses involved in running it also grew. We had a membership fee by this time as we put out a little magazine. There was also the cost of printing the graduation certificates and various other expenses, some connected with the ceremonies at which the certificates were presented. I began to feel that the inescapable practicalities of this undertaking, the decisions involved, especially the increasingly prominent role of money and membership fees, were leading me away from the spirit of my commitment to Chan. My partner in the venture, a forceful lady formerly a Captain in the Salvation Army, often took a different view from mine. I therefore decided it was right to end the school.

More clearly than ever now I see that this was one more example of what I have been aware of ever since I made my commitment and received Chan's promise that together we would serve Spirit. In this work my only possible partnership is with him.

Not only my teaching methods but my mediumship, too, was different, in that Chan's communication through me was not of the personal nature that was normal with many mediums. I have even been told by sitters with some of these others that it was like having their loved ones back again, like having a conversation with them. That was not my way and Chan explained to me that my psychological make-up did not lend itself to this kind of submission to another mind. The only person I ever allowed to control me was Chan. I do not fully understand this, but I do not think I could ever be hypnotised either, because my insistence on maintaining my own identity and my respect for my own freedom is very pronounced. The only time I ever tried was with a friend who practised hypnosis. With her I never let go of my own will; I always knew that I could stop if I wanted to.

Knowing this about the nature of my mediumship, I had some misgivings over what an elderly widower told me. He used to sit with me regularly for some years after the death of his wife, Katie, and would tell me after these sittings how wonderful it had been, that Katie had spoken directly to him, and this made me uncomfortable. However, his need was so great that I did not have the heart to refuse. When he became more frail he went to live at Charterhouse where I visited him almost every week for two or three years until he died. This ancient charity, housed in a very beautiful building on its original site in the City of London, interested me greatly. Suttons Hospital in Charterhouse, to give it its correct name, was founded in 1611 by Thomas Sutton. Its purposes were twofold. One was 'to educate up to forty poor scholars'. This has since become a famous public school and has long outgrown the London premises; it moved to Godalming in 1872. The other purpose was to be 'a hospital for up to eighty elderly men in need of charity.' The eighty men accommodated are 'retired sea captains' – as mentioned in the original documents – or retired priests, actors or other men whose life's work has not provided them with provision for their old age. My friend was a solicitor.

At his funeral, an orthodox ceremony but conducted with real feeling, after the benediction I suddenly knew that Katie was there. It was as if, with this knowing which I had, she took me by the hand, and thanking me for everything I had done, said, 'I am going to take care of him now.'

To me, that was a real assurance that I had not been deceiving myself, that she really had been there talking to him. I have never had that experience with anyone else because I do not take to different controls. I know that Chan is right when he says I am psychologically unfit for opening up to changing personalities. He never attempted to embark on this in my training because he was only concerned with what I could develop to the high standard required to satisfy him.

The comfort that I was able to bring to widowers sometimes led to proposals of marriage. I was never seriously tempted to consider these, even those which would have provided me with material comfort and security, but I did enjoy the lavish bouquets of roses which one suitor sent to me over quite a long period of time.

During these years which I think of as the second half of my life, when Janet and I had become lifelong friends and companions, my travels took me further afield than in those early days.

Through Chan's guidance – there is nothing personal about this – I was often able to help people. At Belgrave Square (I think it was in the early 1960's) I met a young man from South Africa who was in London to study law. He had fallen on hard times and this was an extremely difficult period in his life, so from time to time I gave him a sitting for which I knew he did not have the money to pay. He used to come to the flat in Richmond Green where Janet and I were living at that time and I know that he gained a great deal from the guidance which Chan afforded him through me. Before returning to South Africa, after thanking me profusely, he said he would never forget what I had done for him and that if ever he was able to repay me, he would.

Some years later, towards the end of the 1960's, we

received a letter inviting us to spend a holiday, at his expense, in South Africa where he and his wife would be delighted to do everything they could to make our stay enjoyable. He was well off now, with a beautiful house outside Johannesburg, and when the dates were arranged in regard to my work and for Janet to have a month's leave, he sent us our air tickets.

After an extremely pleasant week in their home in Johannesburg he had to go to Cape Town on business. He hired a car and took us with him, installing us in a hotel in Cape Town where he left us to enjoy two weeks' holiday on our own before returning with him to Johannesburg. That was a truly wonderful time.

To our host, I was above all else a medium, one who had helped him in a remarkable way, and he was very keen to show me off to his friends. Of course, I felt obliged to give sittings when asked, so as usual I found myself singing for my supper, though I did this willingly as he had been so very generous. When the time came for us to leave he tried to make our stay permanent by offering Janet a job at a very much higher salary than she was earning in the Civil Service in England, together with a rent-free bungalow in the grounds of their home in Johannesburg. For my part, I would be available for anyone who needed my mediumistic gift.

On the surface it seemed a great temptation but deep down we both knew that this was not right for us. I could never be so beholden to anyone, much less allow my mediumship to fall under the influence of anyone but Chan.

This was the second time in my life when I might have made my home outside England. I had a cousin, quite a bit older than I, who was secretary to Lord Northcliffe at the

Daily Mail. When she and her mother emigrated to Canada I was still quite a young child. My aunt asked my mother if she could adopt me and take me also. I wished very much to go with them and it would certainly have seemed to my advantage at the time to have a more normal home life, but my mother decided against it – again, with hindsight, I am sure under spiritual direction.

Janet did not accompany me the first time I was invited to Amsterdam. It was after I had been demonstrating at the S.A.G.B. that a Dutch gentleman approached me to ask if I would visit him and his wife; he had a friend who could see auras and he thought I would be interested. There must have been something I liked about this man because without hesitation I said yes, I would be very happy to go. A week-end was arranged, he sent me my ticket, but on the plane, sitting with a Japanese either side of me, I began to wonder what I was doing. I thought I must have been mad to accept so hastily, and why had I not insisted that Janet should come with me?

My host, an extremely wealthy man, was head of a major Dutch pasta firm and as we drove through the city I saw his family name flashing out in lights on more than one impressive building. To my great relief and delight his wife and I hit it off immediately and from the moment I met her I began to enjoy myself.

When my plane touched down it was already well into the dinner hour and by the time I had been driven to his home, introduced to his wife and had a little time to relax, it was already late. They took me to a restaurant on the waterfront which was just about to close as we arrived. For him, they opened it up again, rekindled the stove in the centre of the room and produced a marvellous dinner. It was very late indeed when we finally emerged. As we walked the few paces to the car, the waterfront stretched before us, deserted, in the dark. Until the car lights were switched on! In their beam we saw hundreds and hundreds of rabbits running around, chasing each other and playing together; the water's edge, a sort of strand, was alive with rabbits.

I shall hold that picture in my mind until my dying day. I have a thing about rabbits. The first one I ever saw was on the farm where Philip and Derek were evacuated during the war when I was charmed to see this furry creature, new to me, sitting up and washing its face with its paws.

Next day my Dutch friends took me to see the man they had told me about who polished semi-precious stones and made very beautiful jewellery. That first visit to Amsterdam was the start of a friendship which lasted over ten years. We looked forward to seeing them when they visited London and Janet and I were invited three times to have a holiday, when we were given a bungalow to ourselves on the family estate with swimming pool, tennis courts and every other amenity. When we wanted to see something of Amsterdam his wife would drive us in and show us the sights. We were very sad when he died and, some years later, his wife.

One Sunday, when I had been demonstrating at a church in Bromley, a man came up to me afterwards and asked to speak to me privately. Declaring that the quality of my work had greatly impressed him, he asked if I would consider making a professional visit to Australia. Looking back, I cannot imagine what induced me to agree, certainly not without going into the conditions of such a tour much more thoroughly. But I have been dedicated to doing whatever I am asked to do in service and have never attached importance to what such service might mean to me personally. All expenses were to be paid and, naive as I was in regard to my personal interests, in my innocence, I accepted.

Janet could not get time off from her work to come with me this time, as she had telescoped two years' leave for our South African trip. If she had been with me, the outcome might have been different. I do not know. As it was another friend accompanied me, but one with whom I was not really in tune on a deep level. I know, and I should have known then, that temperamentally I am not suited to be close to anyone with the exception of my dear Janet.

From the moment I arrived in Australia until the time I left I was working almost constantly. The distances were enormous; my demonstrations might be hundreds of miles apart, and I was rushed from one place to another without a break. Often we did not stop even for a meal and I would be lucky if I got a cup of tea. In one place I worked in the University with extremely demanding though enthusiastic audiences. I was guest of honour on radio programmes and did three television programmes in a row. An enormous amount of interest and publicity was aroused, leading inexorably to ever-increasing pressure on me.

But no-one had told me how beautiful Australia is: the blue mountains, brilliantly colourful birds, kangaroos and other fascinating animals, the vegetation – all these were exquisite. One happy memory of this tour is of a small place right on the coast. In an hour I had free I went down to the edge of the shore and just stood there peacefully drinking in the beauty, the sea looked so gentle. The first wave came with such force, it knocked me off my feet!

I dearly wanted to see the Opera House in Sydney. My host promised me a day off but it never came. I never had any free time there at all. Even on the day of my departure he got me to the airport only just in time to have a rushed meal before boarding the plane. At the last minute an envelope was pushed into my hand. When I looked inside much later, I saw that it contained the equivalent of the fee I would receive for one sitting at home.

I arrived back in England a nervous wreck and within two or three days went down with shingles. Before I had properly recovered I suffered a severe and prolonged attack of iritis. I really did feel terribly ill. On top of this my bladder trouble flared up. It had been an intermittent discomfort but never so severe as this. I attribute my collapse – it really was a collapse – to this Australian tour, because I had absolutely no resistance left and I was very much more ill than the conditions warranted.

Some time after all this, perhaps a year later, I started passing blood, but ignored it. The following year, 1976, after a pretty strenuous week at a Summer School in Torquay, I had a severe blood loss which, on my return home, took me to the doctor. 'How long,' she demanded, 'has this been going on?' When I told her, 'About a year,' she was outraged. 'Why the so-and-so did you not come before?' That was on a Friday. She had me in Charing Cross Hospital on the following Tuesday where I was told there was something septic in my bladder.

On Thursday they treated this by cauterising it, not surgery, but I was by now extremely ill. I regarded the biopsy as a routine procedure, however, and thought nothing of it.

I was discharged after a few days, feeling very much better, and was unconcerned when I returned after six weeks for a check-up. I had forgotten all about the biopsy. To my utter shock I was told I had a particularly virulent type of cancer and they wanted me in immediately to operate. Now I had always said that if I ever developed cancer I would not submit to surgery as this so often spreads the growth, so I said I would have to think about. 'Don't think too long,' I was told.

Fortunately my own doctor was very sympathetic. She knew about my mediumship and that I was not in favour of an operation, and she explained to me just what the situation was. 'Your cancer is contained in the bladder,' she said. 'It is most unusual to be so contained. It will be like having a tooth out. If you don't, it won't kill you for a very long time but it will become extremely uncomfortable, and so unnecessarily.'

I trusted her and what she said made sense so I went back into hospital and had the operation.

I was so *angry* that I had this cancer. I simply could not accept that this had happened to me. As I lay there in my hospital bed I knew that countless people were sending me healing, powerful healers, and I felt nothing, absolutely nothing at all, I was so wrapped around in this anger. I had a night nurse who hated my guts. The feeling was mutual and one night I was feeling so low, I don't think I have ever, before or since, felt so low as I did then. It was a black night physically as well as emotionally and as I lay there, suddenly – I don't know why – I saw myself on the platform and I heard myself saying, 'Everything we experience has its purpose, its meaning, and we are never without God's love.' And then I saw myself as I was now, riddled with anger and resentment, and I said to myself, 'You hypocrite! It's all right when it's not happening to you, but when it does, it's a very different story.'

What then swept over me – I can only call it penance, because I had not realised, I really had not. And from that moment it was as if I was enveloped in a wonderful cloud of love. It wrapped me round and lifted me up. I have never experienced it quite like that before or since. Sometimes when I am very low I long for that moment again, but it has never come.

But that was the end of my cancer.

CHAPTER 15

First publication of Chan's trance talks. Some memories of Ivy at The College of Psychic Studies. Reflections on Chan's influence and its effects.

My experience of having cancer was one of those landmarks in life which stand out so clearly in memory although I recovered completely and never looked back. Happy recollections are not usually so dramatic.

I have never courted publicity and the way in which I have always worked under Chan's direction has sometimes seemed to me to have the opposite effect. But one of the greatest joys was when Ralph Rossiter asked if I would agree to the transcripts of my Chan lectures at the Spiritualist Association of Great Britain being published in a booklet. First appearing in 1970 as *Trance Talks by "Chan"*, it was re-named *Journey Beyond* and has just had its seventh reprinting, now being a title of LIGHT Publishing at the College of Psychic Studies. But what is so gratifying to me is to realise the help which Chan's wisdom, reaching out in this form, has been to so many people. I know this from the innumerable letters I receive and it was in order to make Chan's teaching methods available to a much wider range of students than I could ever meet personally that I wrote my book on mediumship.

I had already been working for some years at the College

of Psychic Studies at the time I went to Australia. It must have been about 1970, at a conference in Bristol to discuss ways of improving mediumship where I was on the platform and he was in the audience, that I first met Paul Beard, one of the most notable of all the presidents of the College.

Like his father and his uncles before him, he had a lifelong interest in mediumship. They were all to some extent gifted in this way; one uncle had been a professional medium and his father had founded the London Spiritual Mission in Pembridge Place. Paul's study of mediumship and communication with higher levels of consciousness, above all of the guidance available from these higher levels if only we would attune ourselves to receive it, was a dominating interest of his life, one aspect of which found its expression in three books he wrote which have become classics in their field. His heart was very much in the better training of mediums and he was determined to provide the conditions in which he felt they could do their best work and, above all, not spoil their gift by overworking.

During the Bristol conference, as always when speaking on this subject, I stressed not only the need for total discipline and the putting aside of all personal feelings or idiosyncrasies, but also what I have called in my book the mechanics of mediumship. Just as singers need to master vocal technique, and learn how to control their voice so that they can produce at will any note within their particular range, so mediums need to understand their psychic mechanism as an instrument which should be under *their* control. Only on this foundation can they be sure of relaying with accuracy whatever may be communicated through them. Furthermore, only by being in complete control of their mechanism will they be able to distinguish, for instance, what they may be picking up from the mind of a sitter from what unmistakably emanates from the discarnate level. This is an area of confusion which has given rise to a great deal of criticism of mediumship as such, whereas the fault is in the inadequate training.

Needless to say these strictures, as on other occasions, did not go down too well but I could see, sitting at the back of the hall, one man nodding approvingly. This was Paul Beard.

Not long before this conference I had read and admired an article he had written for *Psychic News*, so when the official business of the conference came to an end I went over and spoke to him. This impulse was obviously mutual. On the spot Paul asked me if I would come and work at the College, inviting me to take classes there as well as private sittings, to which I gladly agreed. Paul would have liked me to give up my other work and devote myself exclusively to the College, but this I could not do. My commitment was to Chan and to serve wherever that might lead me without any restriction whatever. I knew that, however reluctantly, I had to decline Paul's very tempting offer. I did not even have to ask Chan.

Nevertheless, that was the beginning of one of the most rewarding chapters in my life, one which continued without a break. I had my own room for private sittings which were spaced out to suit me without any need for strain (as are the sittings of all mediums working at the College). In my classes there I was able to bring my students up to higher standards and my Chan lectures reached a much wider audience. In those years people used to be turned away at the door and on more than one occasion the queue continued outside the College and some way down the street.

The culmination of this care is one of my happiest and proudest recollections. To celebrate my eightieth birthday the College gave me a magnificent party. As well as friends and colleagues from my professional life, all my family were invited; my sons with their wives and two cousins, all of whom were seeing this side of my life for the first time. I knew there was to be a presentation because I had been asked to sit for my portrait. Determined to have a dress worthy of the occasion, I found one after much searching. In oyster chiffon, it had mother of pearl on the bodice, I remember, and batwing sleeves. An incident on my way there stays vividly in my mind. At traffic lights in South Kensington the hired car in which I was being driven came to a halt exactly beside one in which the Queen was travelling and I found myself sitting next to her with only the sides of the two cars between us. I was close enough to admire her flawless complexion as she sat looking straight ahead, exuding serenity. She really did impress me very much.

At the College the lecture hall had been transformed with masses of flowers. The presentation was to have been made by Rosamond Lehmann, but by a mishap the taxi she had ordered never arrived and she came late to the party. Rosamond, a famous novelist in her day, was for years Vice President of the College. Shattered by the tragic early death of her daughter which overnight turned her rich social and professional life into a mockery and left her empty and desolate, it was only when she was led to realise the possibility of communication and, to her lasting joy, to experience it, that she felt able to take up her life again, enduring with equanimity the ridicule of many of her former friends. It was in this later period that we at the College came to know and love her.

So it was Paul Beard who made the presentation. As well as the portrait, he handed me an illuminated scroll of commendation and an envelope with a cheque.

Overwhelmed – quite overcome for a moment by this very sincere and quite tangible loving expression of appreciation, I was speechless, temporarily at a loss as to how to respond. Suddenly I thought of Stanley and how he was always against sending flowers to funerals. Whenever he saw a cortège passing in the street he used to say, 'I'd rather have my flower money now.' I told them this, and added, 'I feel as if I am having my flower money now!'

That broke the ice and I was able to express something of the gratitude I felt for the evident warmth and affection of everyone present.

The portrait was by Honor Earl. After it was finished she attended a lecture I gave and told me afterwards that she did not think she had caught the expression; it was not lively enough, and she asked me to sit for her again. The second portrait is the one which is now at the College and I have the first at home.

Perhaps neither quite captures the real me, both tend to be rather too pretty – that, at least, is the general opinion – but this just brings home to me yet again the realisation that my long association with Chan has imbued me with that detachment so essential to the work he has tried to do through me. Nothing could detract from my appreciation and enjoyment of the personal warmth and friendship shown to me, but I had by this time got over any desire for publicity.

So I was in fact unmoved when, for a book which appeared in 1993, *The Best of British Men & Women*, I was chosen as one of the six best women mediums featured alongside half a dozen of the selected best men.

Throughout my professional life I have collaborated with researchers and agreed to take part in innumerable radio and television programmes, though with increasingly less enthusiasm. I never took kindly to guessing cards. To me, the psychic gift is meant to be used for a purpose. Often, listening to the obligatory sceptics on media programmes I have been reminded of what Stanley said in the early days, that at first what impressed him most was the inadequacy of the sceptics' arguments. But I have been privileged to work with a rare few with whom I gladly cooperated. There was a period when a small group of members of The Society for Psychical Research had regular sittings with me in my home. And I remember Professor Maxwell Cade who was researching brainwave patterns in differing states of consciousness. He had an instrument to measure these in some way and I willingly allowed him to use it on me when I was in trance. He told me afterwards that mine was the deepest trance state he had come across, measured, if I understood him correctly, by the length of time it took me to return to normal consciousness.

My life's work as a medium has been based on putting myself, my personal concerns, completely out of the way. I am quite unaccustomed to introspection nor have I ever had any use for psychological probing or analysis, but looking back I can see that I have become an entirely different person from my younger self. Indeed, I am emerging more of a stranger to myself than when I began.

As a child I knew no affection except that of my mother which remained largely unexpressed as she was always worn out with the struggle to support us. Apart from her, no-one even called me by my first name. I was always 'that Fitzpatrick child' – when not 'that *awful* Fitzpatrick child!' – from the earliest years I can remember and in my efforts to keep my end up I made myself very unpopular. The one exception was that teacher who spoke to me kindly when I had a migraine and gave me a note for the crèche. I would have done anything for her and in later life we kept up a friendship until she died.

No doubt my lonely childhood helped to develop the fortitude and hardihood which enabled me to cope with a great many physical difficulties in my life, not least of which were the hardships of travelling in wartime (not to mention sleepless nights in air raid shelters) and the endurance to carry on with my work, sometimes in most adverse conditions and even in spite of major illness.

As the years go by I feel a deeper bond than ever with my mother and with Stanley, both of whom, as I can see even more clearly now, did not have much happiness in their lives. I sometimes think of Stanley at Philip's bed in hospital when we thought our son was dying, then leading me away with the words, 'We can do more good if we go home and pray.' How did Stanley know that this was the right thing to do when I was dead against it and tried to persuade him to stay? He must have received direct guidance, sensitive man that he was. I like to think – as indeed I have come to know – that he and my mother are now aware of how far I myself have travelled because of all the devotion and all the help they gave me. Without them, my life story would indeed have been very different.

Stanley once asked Chan what one could expect immediately after physical death. Chan told him that this was individual but that in a general way familiarity was the operative word, adding that although individuals in the body are not always aware they are about to die, their spiritual companions always know. He added that not all spirits make contact with mediums through the astral levels. If they want to be there to meet their loved ones they have to be taught how to modify and decrease their vibration.

This is one of many recollections which come to mind and which illustrates the thoroughness of Stanley's' investigation.

Following from those very early days, the slow process of melting into Chan that was an essential part of his ministry through me had many ups and downs. Gradually I came to recognise my own intrusions, my own ideas that seemed to be percolating into what Chan wanted to convey and this was gradually but gently overlaid by a greater control and command from him. I can see a very subtle balance here. My life experiences and what I learned from dealing with them made me an altogether more capable person and therefore a much better instrument for Chan than when in my puppet role of that early period when Stanley's enthusiasm was my only motivation. But as I became a more mature person my will had consciously to be relinquished to Chan's guidance for the purpose of our service together.

Though quite unaware at the time, I see now how these hidden influences from Chan, gradually percolating into my physical consciousness, were moulding me, producing a growing self-reliance and mental capability instead of the old immaturity and insecurity, making me into an altogether more useful instrument through whom Chan could operate.

I think only once have I really rebelled and turned for a while away from my work with Chan, although without at the time realising that this had happened. Suddenly I was brought up abruptly against circumstances which compelled me to see that there was only one way forward for me and that was back to our partnership. This was in regard to my school for mediums. The fact of having accepted a partner on the physical plane made an insidious change in me, in that whereas I had always taken my guidance from Chan, now we were taking decisions and that spiritual guidance was edged out. One way in which this made itself felt was that we fell out, not personally but clashing in our decisions. Unpleasant as this was, it forced me to realise that not only could I not avoid being Chan's medium but that this was what I wanted from my life above all else.

I feel I can truly say now that I have achieved complete separation between the personal me and my mediumship. I suppose that is an achievement. I am glad when people say I (meaning Chan) have helped them, but glad in a detached way. I now have this inner note, an inner chord, which tells me if I have done the best I could. That is what matters to me.

CHAPTER 16
CHAN. Looking back.

It is obvious by now that Chan has been the ruling influence in my life. He is implicit in everything I have written, but people often find it difficult to understand the difference between our spiritual partnership, which has been unbroken, and my personal difficulties and times of trial when I have told them that he has never, ever, intervened in my personal life. Sometimes I have found his detachment a little hard; he has often seemed to expect so much from me. On the human level I am aware that my life has been lonely. I have never, for instance, experienced a true depth of human love.

I have had times of rebellion when I have gone my own way and shut Chan out and he has waited patiently, with no reproach, for me to return. When I have come back – as of course I always did – he has quietly picked up the pieces and we have continued from where we left off. He has never withheld criticism when he has thought it necessary but has always, no less firmly for all the gentleness of his manner, pointed out where I was failing our work together and insisted that I make the necessary changes, whether in my mediumship or in aspects of my private life which were detracting from the effectiveness of my work.

So gently did Chan guide me that I was barely aware of it at the time. It is only now, when I look back on my life, that I see clearly how wonderfully supportive he has always been, how remarkably understanding. Without ever conveying directly what he was doing, he has understood completely just what I needed at any particular time and made sure that the appropriate and necessary experience came my way. Now I am so close to him that I seldom make a mistake.

Over the years we have built up a very organised and methodical partnership on a purely mental level.

Most people have seen their guides but I have never seen Chan. He told me that I would not see him. I do not know why. Somehow or other I know that he is there and that I do not need to see him. When on one occasion I said to him, 'Everyone else sees their guide, why can't I?' he simply replied that it was not necessary, adding, 'When you do see me you will know that this journey is over and we shall go on together.' That, I feel sure, was a very special promise even if I do not yet fully understand it. When the time comes for me to go I have no doubt that its significance will be revealed and I shall know why I have never yet seen him.

What I do have is a kind of mental picture, a powerful inner sensing and this is why, for me, the portrait of Chan done by a psychic artist is not a true likeness. How could it be? His spirit, his being, is too great to be pinned down in one finite likeness. However, how he cooperated in its production is interesting.

Chan has been the spiritual guide of a great many people who have attended my groups at the College of Psychic

Studies, many of whom have become devoted to him. A good many years ago, and quite unknown to me, about six of these arranged a sitting with a well-known psychic artist and collectively sent up a mental request that, if possible, Chan would convey a picture of himself to the artist, of course without revealing their intention to her.

One of those present told me afterwards that the psychic artist suddenly remarked that a Chinese gentleman had come in saying that the group had specially invited him. This was typical Chan, half tongue-in-cheek; he would never miss such an opportunity. My group recognised the personality; they could identify Chan's unmistakable presence. Then the psychic said, 'He is telling me that he is not really anything to do with you (the group), his connection is with a very dear friend, but he wants you to know that he did hear your request and would like to make this contribution to your very kind thought.' The result is the picture which since then has appeared on the cover of my books.

My life did not get easier as the years went by, but always there was this support in the background.

When people know you as a medium, they do not really know *you*. They tend to think that mediums are exempt from life's normal trials and tribulations as their guides must surely warn them of approaching disasters and so make it possible to avoid them. The truth is very different. Mediumship is just one of the paths being travelled by the spirit which has its own lessons to learn, its own weaknesses to overcome. The spiritual understanding and fellowship which develop through mediumship do not make life any easier. On the contrary, this seems in fact to multiply the difficulties. It complicated my domestic situation and often made my material life very difficult to deal with and even to bear, but there is no medium I know who has not had a period in their life when, beset with difficulties, they have not known which way to turn.

Yet, if they remain true to their dedicated purpose and open to guidance offered from a higher level, difficulties and apparent setbacks do not end in disaster. This has been my experience right from the time I committed myself to serve with Chan. The outcome of my nearly fatal illness in Exeter was a most striking example of this, another was the guidance Stanley received to go home and pray when Philip was thought to be dying.

Those in spirit can only work in our world through us. This often causes confusion and makes people wonder why help was not afforded in a given situation. The spiritual realms can only help us in our physical lives through those humans who make themselves available for such service by being open to guidance from higher levels. Again, this was clearly borne out by my Exeter experience. I was at the mercy of people deaf to guidance from these levels until, *just at the moment when I was ready,* that kindly nurse was prompted – out of the blue, as it seemed – to offer to take me in and look after me, a person entirely unknown to her.

Such spiritual help may be life-saving but it does not prevent the physical pain. The physical has its own reality and its consequences are not set aside.

I have often thought about the pain I caused to Stanley when I refused to cancel touring engagements when he was on leave from the army. One such occasion, when I was in Wales when Stanley came home on embarkation leave, he took especially badly, maintaining that I should have cancelled my bookings and come home to spend this time with him. I recalled our commitment after Chan had repeated insistently, 'Do you really mean you are going to put this work before *anything*' and we swore that we did. When I reminded Stanley of this he objected, 'But Chan didn't mean that, there wasn't a war on then.'

I have sometimes wondered if I did the right thing, causing Stanley pain at such a critical time for him, but I had given my word and that was that.

Another thing I have learnt is that communication is never wasted from the spirit realm. When it has served its purpose it is not repeated. How well I recollect our early venture into table-tapping and those first results of our experiment, when my mother confirmed so many facts we received which were unknown to either of us. This success so aroused the enthusiasm of Stanley, and even of me, that there was no question but that he would seriously continue with our efforts and his researches. We never again had anything meaningful through the table.

This unwillingness from the spirit realm to manifest when their purpose has been served sometimes lies behind the breaking-off or cessation of personal communications. While every instance is individual to those concerned, once the bereaved have received evidence that their loved ones continue in another dimension, it is sometimes more helpful to encourage them to search further, and more deeply, than to provide repeated communication.

When hearing of my own difficulties and disappointments, people have asked why Chan did not protect me, showing their lack of understanding of spiritual law in this respect. Chan cannot interfere in the way I handle my life. I must make my own decisions and if, in anything where my mediumship is concerned, I say 'yes' he will do his best to assist in producing whatever my agreement is demanding from me. But if I weakly say 'yes', or my judgement is poor, the quality of my work falls below its proper standard and I myself suffer the physical effects of subjecting my body to strain.

While I have never done anything that Chan has asked me not to, I have on occasion been extremely tired and I know that this always affects my work. When I am tired, it is as though Chan has difficulty in finding the words in my brain. I have always known when this is happening, and it is as if Chan is telling me that I am doing too much, that I must moderate my work. When this happens I have always tried very hard not to take on anything which is extra to the work which has already been planned. That work I have always been able to do satisfactorily. The trouble comes when I do not respect my natural capacity and agree to taken on extra commitments because people ask me to, when I should have learnt so say no. I have always suffered when I allow myself to take on more than I should. My worst experience of this was after my gruelling tour of Australia. My health collapsed from the strain and I succumbed to successive serious illnesses in the years which followed my return.

In retrospect, one of the most amazing things about the whole of my training, although I did not recognise it at the time, was how beautifully organised it was. I still sometimes wish that I could have become a singer, wish that it had been possible for me to have my voice professionally trained. Lack of money made sure that such a course was out of the question and perhaps even this was part of the plan. Looking back one cannot avoid the conclusion that from my earliest years those in the spirit world had their own ideas for me.

Everything connected with spiritual reality seems to come such a long way ahead. I do not mean that those from that world tell you this or that is going to happen but that the things to which they refer often seem to make no sense at the time. Subsequently, however, as these patterns unfold, those other factors of which you had no knowledge or understanding when they were given to you, start to reveal themselves and you can glimpse their meaning. Most people I have spoken to would agree. I can only think that this is a kind of spiritual preparation for the events before they take place on the physical plane. Without our conscious knowledge or understanding we are being helped in advance to meet certain challenges which lie ahead in our path. My mentors in spirit must have known about the war which was coming, with the hardships and problems that it would inevitably bring. I see now that both beforehand and as the war with its many reverses was being fought, my preparation for what I myself would have to face was meticulously thorough, but because it came a step at a time I was not aware of what was happening.

So here, yet again, this wonderful caring, this perfect timing. Always my spirit friends have provided what I needed in order to be able to carry on. While one is immersed in the misery of the physical event it is difficult to register this spiritual care but for me it has been like chapters in a book.

Time and time again, when I have felt as if I had reached the end of my endurance, something has occurred, miraculously as it would seem, that has lifted me up and taken me out of the situation.

How can I express my appreciation of my dear Chan? I do not mean his philosophy which has been invaluable to so many people, but the wonderfully understanding person. Despite all that he is and represents, he somehow conveys a sense of humility, not in any Uriah Heep sense but in the unfailingly tranquil way in which he encourages and leads. There is nothing pushing or demanding in his approach, just a gentle persuasion that is inherent in all that he tries to do. Looking back I can see how wisely, yet how simply, he guided me, both on major issues and on details that might have seemed at the time to be of no importance.

When I reflect on this I realise how extraordinarily fortunate I have been and it makes me wonder what I have done to deserve it. Chan has been more than a guide, he has been a friend who has known all my weaknesses, all my problems and sometimes my heartaches, without ever commenting on them. He has never talked about my character, nor has he ever mentioned incidents of a domestic or personal nature, but he has always been there. Through our work together he has gently led me away from any hint of self-absorption, so that in our partnership I became quite single-minded and recognised that what we did together was entirely separate from my personal life.

Chan has been endlessly patient with explanations of anything relating to my mediumship, but he has never discussed anything personal concerning my life. From an early age I have always been aware of a part of me trying to reach upwards, a striving towards something sensed as above my head. Gradually, over the years, through my endeavour to understand spiritual law and what at-one-ment with God really meant, I became more in touch with my own spirit. This was separate from my mediumship; there was a part of me not in communication with Chan but which was in touch with something else above and beyond what was around me. Intangible and impossible to put into words, it was a kind of instinctive knowing which saved me on many occasions.

How I would dearly love to talk to someone like Chan about me, the person! But I have accepted wholeheartedly that because of the nature of our relationship this is quite impossible. Yet always patiently through the years, dealing with the innumerable incidents as they occurred, Chan has been such a wonderful support to me in a way that I have never truly appreciated until now when I come to reflect on my life.

As I look back I can see how, unknown to me, my path has been mapped out from the beginning. I believe that this is true of a great many more people than are aware of it, and that if people would only reflect on their lives they would see their own pattern and perceive a continuing thread of meaning in their experiences as these unfold. By doing so and consciously cooperating with this pattern, they would become active partners in the underlying purpose of their lives.

End

Some other titles from LIGHT PUBLISHING

SPIRITUAL REALISATION: INNER VALUES IN EVERYDAY LIFE
Communications by CHAN, spirit guide of Ivy Northage
CHAN'S suggestions for handling life's problems carry spiritual authority but are never over-assertive. A book to treasure.
£7.50 paperback, ISBN 0 903336 21 9

MEDIUMSHIP MADE SIMPLE by Ivy Northage
Widely regarded as one of the classic texts on practical mediumship. Ivy Northage draws on forty years as medium and teacher, giving clear descriptions of psychic development and its practical applications.
£7.99 paperback, ISBN 0 903336 19 7

JOURNEY BEYOND Trance Talks by Chan, the Guide of Ivy Northage
One of the best, clearest and most convincing accounts of the journey through physical 'death' to the realms beyond. Chan's concise descriptions answer many of our deepest questions about the meaning of life and the passage through 'death'.

THE CHANGELING by Murry Hope
A new title. This extraordinary – unique – autobiography from the author of 20 books on extra-terrestrial lives is illuminated by touches of humour and a wry, perceptive wit. LIGHT Publishing is proud to have been chosen to publish this most personal of all this popular author's books.
£9.99 ISBN 0 903336 31 6

INSIGHT AND INTUITION by Julie Soskin
Julie's eagerly-awaited manual on psychic and spiritual development is virtually a do-it-yourself manual on cosmic consciousness. Exercises in each chapter help the reader to absorb the essence of what is written and integrate it into their daily lives.
£9.99 paperback, ISBN 0 903336 14 6

TRANSFORMATION by Julie Soskin
The fourth channelled work by Julie Soskin reveals the enormous shift now occurring in the evolution of humanity and the changes this will bring in our lives.
£6.99 paperback, ISBN 0 903336 24 3

IN TOUCH WITH RAYNOR C. JOHNSON by Sheila Gwillam
With a Foreword by Paul Beard. Wisdom and spiritual insight from a renowned scientist, author and spiritual philosopher.
£8.99 paperback, ISBN 0 903336 15 4

THE NEW SCIENCE OF THE SPIRIT by David A. Ashe
An exciting new approach providing a framework for the universe in which the laws of physics and the laws of the spirit become one.
£9.95 hardback, ISBN 0 903336 56 1
£6.99 paperback, ISBN 0 903336 55 3

PRINCIPLES OF THE UNIVERSE by Keith Casburn
Communications from a source beyond the time frame of our solar system; the multidimensional nature of being; how to become the spiritual beings we really are.
£6.99 paperback, ISBN 0 903336 28 6

IZARIS by Keith Casburn
Communications from Izar, one of the second magnitude stars in our universe, tells us how we relate vibrationally to stars and galaxies, and the demands this makes on us mentally, emotionally and physically.
£8.99 paperback, ISBN 0 903336 12 X

SOUL TREK by Julie Gale
A channelled book tracing the soul's evolution from the Source, through physical incarnation and beyond. Sheds new light on subjects such as group souls, twin souls and reincarnation.
£8.99 paperback, ISBN 0 903336 26 X

SOULWORK: FOUNDATIONS FOR SPIRITUAL GROWTH
by Sue Minns
The College's answer to those unable to attend CPS classes. This 166-page tabulated Workbook and the six audio cassettes are based on Sue Minns' Foundation Course at the College of Psychic Studies. They offer step-by-step guidance for your own inner unfoldment, providing direction along the way. Graduated lessons cover:
Breathing, Meditation, The Aura, Chakras, Healing, Psychic Energy, Body/Mind, Inner Child and Soul, Karma and Reincarnation.
£39.99 Workbook & six audio-cassettes, ISBN 0 903336 16

The College of Psychic Studies
16 Queensberry Place
South Kensington
London SW7 2EB
Telephone: 0171 589 3292/3
Fax: 0171 589 2824
E-mail: cpstudies@aol.com
Website: www.psychic.studies.org.uk